# Become a Friend of the *Mississippi Law Journal*

Today the *Mississippi Law Journal* is funded and operated almost exclusively through student efforts. Increasingly, however, the *Journal* depends on the support of its alumni and friends. You can become a Friend of the *Mississippi Law Journal* by making a tax-deductible contribution to one of the funds listed below. Checks should be made payable to the University of Mississippi Foundation and mailed to Post Office Box 8288, University, Mississippi 38677. *Please indicate on your check to which fund you intend to contribute.*

### Robert C. Khayat Scholarship Endowment

The Robert C. Khayat Scholarship Endowment was established in 1995 to honor the dedicated service of Robert C. Khayat, a *Journal* alumnus, professor of law, and chancellor emeritus of the university. Each year the *Journal* awards the Robert C. Khayat scholarship to a deserving member.

### *Mississippi Law Journal* Endowment

The *Mississippi Law Journal* Endowment exists to ensure the *Journal's* future financial stability. As an entity financially independent of the school of law, the *Journal* depends partially on this endowment to fund its operations.

### *Mississippi Law Journal* Operating Fund

All contributions to the *Mississippi Law Journal's* operating fund help the *Journal* to meet its most immediate needs, including the cost of publication.

# Friends of the *Mississippi Law Journal**

Dr. Guthrie T. Abbott
Mrs. Paula Graves Ardelean
The Honorable Rhesa H. Barksdale
Mr. Ross F. Bass Jr.
Mr. William H. Beck Jr.
Bennett Lotterhos Sulser and Wilson
The Honorable William H. Bizzell
The Honorable Eugene M. Bogen
Mrs. Teri M. Bowie
Mrs. Lorraine Walters Boykin
Mr. John R. Braley IV
Mr. Charles L. Brocato
Mr. Jason W. Burch
Mr. James T. Caldwell
The Honorable Thad Cochran
Mr. Richard G. Cowart
Mr. T. David Cowart
Mr. Frank Crosthwait Jr.
Mr. Arlen B. Coyle
Mr. William M. Deavours
Mrs. Marlane Dove
Mr. W. W. Drinkwater Jr.
Dulin & Dulin Ltd.
Lt. Commander W.J. Dunaway
Dr. Wylene W. Dunbar
Mr. Richard M. Edmonson Sr.
Mr. Herbert C. Ehrhardt
Dr. Martha Jane Ellis
Mr. Roger M. Flynt Jr.
Mr. William M. Gage
Mr. Robert C. Galloway
Mrs. Gretchen L. Gentry
Mr. Eugene B. Gifford Jr.
Mr. Hampton Glover Jr.
Mr. William N. Graham
Mrs. Lillows Ann S. Grayson
Mr. Newt P. Harrison
Mr. Robert H. Hodges
Mr. Jamie G. Houston III
Mr. Gary K. Jones
Mr. W.R. Jones Jr.
Mr. William T. Jones
Mrs. Patricia Fleming Kennedy
Mr. William N. Krucks
The Honorable Tom Stewart Lee
Mrs. Virginia C. Lococo
Mr. Roland Marble Sr.
Mr. M.C. Maxwell
Ms. Lydia H. McIntosh
Mr. Jason N. McNeel
Mr. Joseph R. Meadows
Michael T. & Pauline S. Lewis
Mr. Russell W. Mills
Mr. David W. Mockbee
Mr. H. Dixon Montague
Mr. Dalton M. Mounger

Mrs. Trudy Lumpkin Muench
Mrs. Julie Sneed Muller
Mr. Christopher Tyson Nettles
Mr. James W. O'Mara
The Honorable J. D. Orlansky
Mr. Tom Ostenson
Mr. James A. Peden Jr.
Mr. Leroy D. Percy
Mr. Richard T. Phillips
Mr. Rubel L. Phillips
Mr. Benjamin J. Piazza Jr.
Mr. George B. Pickett Jr.
Mr. C. Michael Pumphrey
Mr. Clayton C. Purdom
Mr. Hollaman M. Raney
Mr. Eric Tyson Ray
Mr. Richard Roberts III
Mr. Lucius F. Sams Jr.
Ms. Lillous A. Shoemaker
Mr. George M. Simmerman Jr.
Mr. Jimmy Sledge Jr.
Mr. W. Marion Smith
Mr. Ronald T. Solberg
Mr. Darrell Solomon
Mr. Arthur D. Spratlin Jr.
Mrs. Patricia L. Stevens
Mr. Phineas Stevens
Mr. Samuel James Stigler
Mrs. Molly Fergusson Stuart
Mrs. Nancy H. Stumberg
Ms. Margaret J. Murphy Sweetland
Mr. Frank W. Trapp
Mr. Clint Douglas Vanderver
Mr. J. P. Varner
Mr. Lawrence D. Wade
Mrs. Michelle Clingan Waits
Mr. Tim Walsh
Mr. George D. Warner Jr.
Mr. Irwin G. Waterman
Mr. Louis H. Watson Jr.
Mr. Walker L. Watters
Dr. Robert A. Weems
Mr. Eddie C. Williams
Capt. Ronald J. Wojdyla

*As of September 1, 2011*

The *Mississippi Law Journal* is published six times during the academic year. The *Journal*'s editorial and business offices may be contacted via U.S. mail at: Post Office Box 849, University, Mississippi 38677.

Manuscripts: Manuscripts should be submitted electronically to **misslj@olemiss.edu**. Manuscripts should be in 12-point type and double-spaced, in Microsoft Word, WordPerfect, or PDF. Citations should conform to THE BLUEBOOK: A UNIFORM SYSTEM OF CITATION (19th ed. 2010).

Subscriptions: $35.00 per year for domestic subscriptions; $40.00 per year for foreign subscriptions. Single issue: $15.00. Subscriptions are renewed automatically upon expiration unless the subscriber sends a notice of termination.

Change of address: Send address changes directly to the *Mississippi Law Journal*. Include name, new address (including zip code) and old address. Please notify the *Journal* forty-five days in advance to ensure prompt delivery.

Back Issues: Back issues of the *Mississippi Law Journal* may be ordered directly from William S. Hein & Co., Inc., 1285 Main Street, Buffalo, New York 14029-1987. Orders may also be placed by calling William S. Hein & Co., Inc., at (800) 828-7571, via fax at (716) 883-8100 or email to order@wshein.com. Back issues are available in PDF format through HeinOnline.

The *Mississippi Law Journal* is a member of the National Conference of Law Reviews. To offer its contributors complete freedom, the *Journal* assumes no responsibility for the views expressed herein.

# Mississippi Law Journal

Published by Students at the
University of Mississippi School of Law

| VOLUME 81 | 2011 | NUMBER 1 |
|---|---|---|

Copyright © 2011, Mississippi Law Journal, Inc.

*Editor-in-Chief*
BRENT COLE

*Executive Editor*
J. MORGAN STEPHENS

*Executive Articles Editors*
ALAN BAKER
MICHAEL BARBEE
LUKE CANTRELL
ADRIA HERTWIG
LOREN MCRAE

*Business Manager*
WILL CRAVEN

*Executive Supra Editor*
BRITTANY BARTLEY

*Notes & Comments Editors*
ANDREW S. HARRIS
KATE VAN NAMEN

*Mississippi Cases Editor*
PATRICK LOFTON

*Associate Editors*

*Articles Editors*
MICHAEL ATTAWAY
PARKER BERRY
ROBERT CAIN
ROBERT FORD
WES FRANCIS
CASSI FRANKS
KATHLEEN INGRAM
MARY JORDAN KIRKLAND
BRYAN SAWYERS
AUSTIN STOKES

*Mississippi Cases Editors*
CHRISTINE BOCEK
JOHN CARRINGTON
JOSH DANIEL
ANDREW TOMINELLO

*Technical Editor*
APRIL H. KILLCREAS

*Symposium Editor*
JEFFREY BROWN

*Notes & Comments Editor*
ELIZABETH HYDE

Supra *Editors*
ELLIOTT FLAGGS
MATT SITTON

*Faculty Advisors*
DEBORAH H. BELL
JOHN CZARNETZKY
ROBERT A. WEEMS

*Staff Editors*

Stephanie Jordan Bennett
Steven Bentley
Alex Bondurant
Travis Brackin
David Bunt
Susan Ellen Burgin
Emily Carroll
Risher Caves
Tulio D. Chirinos
Laura Elizabeth Collins
Charles Cowan
Sarah Dickey
Erin Doctor
M. Davidson Forester III
Haley Fowler
John Hensley
Whitney Holliday

Holly Hosford
Katherine Kimmel
Mary Kristen Kyle
Meagan Linton
R. Benjamin McMurtray
Grant Mullins
Evan Parrott
Erica Peden
Cody Roebuck
Warren A. Stafford
Emily Logan Stedman
Anna Sweat
Kimberly Thompson
Jack West
Brian Whitman
Michael Williams
Suneisha Williams

## ADMINISTRATIVE OFFICERS OF THE UNIVERSITY OF MISSISSIPPI

DANIEL W. JONES — *Chancellor*
MORRIS H. STOCKS — *Provost and Vice Chancellor for Academic Affairs*
ALICE M. CLARK — *Vice Chancellor for Research and Sponsored Programs*
LARRY D. SPARKS — *Vice Chancellor for Administration and Finance*
WENDELL WEAKLEY — *President and CEO, The University of Mississippi Foundation*
ANDREW P. MULLINS JR. — *Chief of Staff to the Chancellor*
TIMOTHY L. WALSH — *Executive Director of Alumni Affairs*
I. RICHARD GERSHON — *Dean of the School of Law and Professor of Law*

## THE LAW SCHOOL FACULTY

GUTHRIE T. ABBOTT, *Professor Emeritus of Law and Butler, Snow, O'Mara, Stevens and Cannada Lecturer in Law Emeritus*

MICHELE ALEXANDRE, *Assistant Professor of Law*

RICHARD L. BARNES, *Professor of Law and Leonard B. Melvin, Jr. Distinguished Lecturer in Law*

DEBORAH H. BELL, *Professor of Law and Mississippi Defense Lawyers Association Distinguished Lecturer in Law*

WILLIAM W. BERRY III, *Assistant Professor of Law*

PERCY J. BLOUNT, *Research Counsel and Instructor, National Center for Remote Sensing, Air and Space Law*

JOHN R. BRADLEY JR., *Professor of Law*

PHILLIP W. BROADHEAD, *Director, Clinical Appeals Program and Clinical Professor of Law*

CHARLES BROWER II, *Croft Professor of International Law and Jessie D. Puckett, Jr. Lecturer in Law*

MERCER E. BULLARD, *Associate Professor of Law*

LARRY BUSH, *Professor Emeritus of Law*

W. TUCKER CARRINGTON, *Director, Mississippi Innocence Project*

DAVID W. CASE, *Associate Professor of Law*

THOMAS K. CLANCY, *Director of the National Center for Justice and the Rule of Law and Research Professor of Law*

GEORGE C. COCHRAN, *Professor of Law*

AARON S. CONDON, *Professor Emeritus of Law*

BENJAMIN P. COOPER, *Assistant Professor of Law*

JOHN M. CZARNETZKY, *Professor of Law and Mitchell, McNutt, and Sams Lecturer*

DONNA DAVIS, *Associate Professor of Law*

SAMUEL M. DAVIS, *Jamie L. Witten Chair of Law and Government and Professor of Law*

JASON DERRICK, *Acting Assistant Professor of Legal Writing*

D. MICHAEL FEATHERSTONE, *Professor Emeritus of Law*

MOLLY FERGUSSON, *Acting Assistant Professor of Legal Writing*

DON L. FRUGE, *Professor Emeritus and President and CEO Emeritus of the University of Mississippi Foundation*

JOANNE I. GABRYNOWICZ, *Director of the National Remote Sensing, Air and Space Law Center and Research Professor of Law*

KRIS L. GILLILAND, *Director of Law Library and Associate Professor of Law*

CHRISTOPHER R. GREEN, *Assistant Professor of Law*

KAREN O. GREEN, *Professor of Law and Mississippi Defense Lawyers Association Distinguished Lecturer in Law*

MATTHEW R. HALL, *Associate Dean for Academic Affairs, Associate Professor of Law and Jessie D. Puckett, Jr., Lecturer*

DESIREE HENSLEY, *Assistant Professor of Law and Director of Civil Legal Clinic*

MICHAEL H. HOFFHEIMER, *Professor of Law and Mississippi Defense Lawyers Association Distinguished Lecturer in Law*

ROBERT C. KHAYAT, *Chancellor Emeritus and Professor Emeritus of Law*

PATRICIA KRUEGER, *Acting Assistant Professor of Legal Writing and Director of Academic Excellence Program*

DON MASON, *Associate Director of the National Center for Justice and the Rule of Law and Lecturer*

GARY MYERS, *Professor of Law and Associate Dean for Research*

JACK W. NOWLIN, *Associate Professor of Law and Jessie D. Puckett, Jr., Lecturer*

NIKI PACE, *Research Counsel, Mississippi-Alabama Sea Grant*

E. FARISH PERCY, *Associate Professor of Law and Jessie D. Puckett, Jr., Lecturer*

LARRY J. PITTMAN, *Professor of Law and Jessie D. Puckett, Jr., Lecturer*

LISA S. ROY, *Associate Professor of Law and Jessie D. Puckett, Jr., Lecturer*

RONALD J. RYCHLAK, *Professor of Law and Mississippi Defense Lawyers Association Lecturer in Law*

JACQUELINE SERRAO, *Associate Director and Instructor, National Remote Sensing, Air and Space Law Center*

STEPHANIE SHOWALTER-OTTS, *Director of the National Sea Grant Law Center and Adjunct Professor of Law*

HANS P. SINHA, *Director of Prosecutorial Externship Program and Clinical Professor of Law*

CAROLYN ELLIS STATON, *Provost Emeritus and Professor Emeritus of Law*

ROBERT A. WEEMS, *Professor of Law and Butler, Snow, O'Mara, Stevens and Cannada Lecturer in Law*

WILL WILKINS, *Director of the Mississippi Law Research Institute*

C. JACKSON WILLIAMS, *Director of Legal Writing Program and Acting Assistant Professor of Legal Writing*

PARHAM H. WILLIAMS JR., *Dean Emeritus and Professor Emeritus of Law*

# MISSISSIPPI LAW JOURNAL

Published by Students at the
University of Mississippi School of Law

| VOLUME 81 | 2011 | NUMBER 1 |
|---|---|---|

## ACKNOWLEDGEMENTS

*The* Mississippi Law Journal *would like to thank the following individuals for their assistance with this edition:*

MACEY EDMONDSON

KRIS GILLILAND

SUE KEISER

DR. GLORIA KELLUM

BARBARA LAGO

PHILIP LEVY

LANGSTON ROGERS

D. ERIC SCHIEFFER

NEIL WISE

\*All Photographs Included in this Issue
Are Provided Courtesy of the
University of Mississippi

# MISSISSIPPI LAW JOURNAL
Published by Students at the
University of Mississippi School of Law

VOLUME 81     2011     NUMBER 1

## TABLE OF CONTENTS

### DEDICATION CEREMONY SPEECHES

| | |
|---|---|
| CHANCELLOR DANIEL W. JONES............................................................. | 1 |
| REVEREND CURTIS E. PRESLEY III........................................................ | 2 |
| GOVERNOR HALEY R. BARBOUR............................................................... | 5 |
| LIEUTENANT GOVERNOR D. PHILLIP BRYANT............................................ | 6 |
| SENATOR W. THAD COCHRAN................................................................. | 8 |
| SENATOR ROGER F. WICKER................................................................... | 9 |
| CHIEF JUSTICE WILLIAM L. WALLER JR.................................................... | 10 |
| WILLIAM C. TROTTER III...................................................................... | 11 |
| DEAN I. RICHARD GERSHON.................................................................. | 12 |
| JAKLYN L. WRIGLEY............................................................................. | 14 |
| AUBREY B. PATTERSON JR.................................................................... | 15 |
| JOHN R. GRISHAM JR........................................................................... | 18 |
| CHANCELLOR EMERITUS ROBERT C. KHAYAT........................................... | 22 |
| PROVOST MORRIS H. STOCKS................................................................ | 27 |

### TRIBUTES TO CHANCELLOR ROBERT C. KHAYAT

| | |
|---|---|
| DEAN I. RICHARD GERSHON .................................................................. | 35 |
| GOVERNOR WILLIAM F. WINTER............................................................. | 37 |
| DR. DANIEL P. JORDAN......................................................................... | 41 |
| CHARLIE FLOWERS............................................................................... | 47 |
| DEAN EMERITUS PARHAM H. WILLIAMS JR............................................... | 51 |
| JUSTICE REUBEN V. ANDERSON.............................................................. | 55 |
| PROFESSOR ROBERT A. WEEMS.............................................................. | 59 |
| PROFESSOR EMERITUS GUTHRIE T. ABBOTT............................................. | 63 |
| JUDGE S. ALLAN ALEXANDER................................................................. | 67 |
| PROFESSOR DEBORAH H. BELL............................................................... | 71 |

| | |
|---|---|
| Mary Ann Connell............................................................................. | 75 |
| Dr. Carolyn Ellis Staton................................................................... | 83 |
| Dr. Andrew P. Mullins Jr.................................................................. | 87 |
| J. Warner Alford Jr........................................................................... | 91 |
| Chancellor Daniel W. Jones............................................................ | 97 |

# DEDICATION OF THE ROBERT C. KHAYAT LAW CENTER

*April 15, 2011**

### Chancellor Daniel W. Jones

Good afternoon. I am pleased to welcome you to this very special celebration, which marks completion of our magnificent new law center and honors our former chancellor's many contributions to our great university.

Thank you for being here and for accommodating the change of venue dictated by the weather. Though we'll miss the opportunity to enjoy the splendor of the Robert C. Khayat Law Center during the ceremony, we enjoy the splendor of the

---

\* The following is an edited transcript of the dedication ceremony for the Robert C. Khayat Law Center, the home of the University of Mississippi School of Law. The event celebrated the completion of the law center's construction and honored Chancellor Emeritus Robert C. Khayat for his years of service to the university and the school of law.

magnificent Gertrude C. Ford Performing Arts Center, another great result of the remarkable leadership of the man we honor today.

Please join me in thanking the string quartet composed of Dr. Robert Riggs, professor of Music. Others in the string quartet Ms. Valencia Thevenin, Ms. Elizabeth Taylor, both graduate students in Music and Dr. Daniell Mattern, professor of Chemistry for the lovely prelude music provided today. Thank you.

Now would you please stand for the presentation of colors by the university's joint ROTC color guard? Please remain standing for the national anthem by Mr. David Walton, a graduate student in Vocal Performance, and for our invocation to be presented by Reverend Curtis Presley III, pastor of Christ Presbyterian Church and a graduate of our school of law.

### *Reverend Curtis E. Presley III*

Let us pray. Our gracious Heavenly Father, we gather here this afternoon to dedicate a school of law. At one level, a building made out of bricks and stone, a place with halls and classrooms, and offices that will be teaming with all sorts of people. At another level, a place of instruction, a place of learning, a place of hard work for men and women who will have wide impact in the lives of many, many other people for many years. We pray that you will use well this building. We pray that you will produce in this building and from this building people who care not simply about the goods of this world, but who care about the good that they may do their fellow man in this world. People who make livings, as well as people who make lives. We pray even as justice and mercy kiss at the cross of Jesus Christ, so there will be graduates from this place, this new law school, who will be instruments of justice and mercy. Graduates who will take to heart the words of the prophet Micah when he says, "He has told you, O man, what is good; And what does the Lord require of you but to do justice, to love kindness, and to walk humbly with your God." All of these things we pray, in Jesus' name. Amen.

## Chancellor Daniel W. Jones

This truly is a wonderful day, not only for our university and its school of law, but also for a man who has given great effort, immeasurable love, and notable ability to our entire university, including its school of law. His work and devotion have transformed this university, and brought her great admiration and respect. We are here today to honor him and his family, and to publicly express our deep appreciation to them by dedicating our grand new law facility the Robert C. Khayat Law Center.

It took several years for Robert to be persuaded for this to be done. But today, we are celebrating his years of service to our university, and the lives that he and his wife Margaret have led. They have unselfishly given their lives to this university, and we are profoundly grateful to both of them.

Now let's welcome members of the Khayat family to this august occasion. Please stand or wave to us as we call your name. First, of course, we want to welcome Robert and Margaret Khayat. Their daughter Margaret Khayat Bratt and her husband David of Grand Rapids, Michigan. Their son Robert C. Khayat, Jr., and his wife Susannah, and Robert and Margaret's grandchildren Molly, Ben, and Betsey—all of Decatur, Georgia. Susannah's mother, Carol Walker of Atlanta, is with us. Robert's brother Eddie Khayat and his wife Deborah of Nashville. Robert's sister, Edna Boone, and her husband Tom of Ocean Springs. And Robert's sister Kathy Murray of Moss Point. Please let me ask any other family and friends sitting with the Khayat family to stand and let us welcome you now please.

We are pleased to have a college board member with us today, one of our own graduates, Dr. Stacy Davidson and his wife Fay from Cleveland, Mississippi.

Partial funding for this project comes from state support. Would members of the Mississippi legislature please stand and allow us to express our appreciation to you.

We are pleased to have with us a number of state and local elected officials, including members of the judiciary. Would all present and former state and local elected officials please stand and allow us to express appreciation to you.

We are pleased that many of the thousands of members of the law school's alumni chapter and Lamar Order are here for this grand celebration. Would all of our alumni please stand and be recognized. Thank you all for being here.

We are also pleased to have several former law deans with us today. I will ask you to stand as I call your name and we will recognize them together when I have concluded this group. First, Dr. Samuel Davis who served as dean from 1997 to 2010. Dr. Guthrie "Guff" Abbott, the school's interim dean from 1985 to 1987. Dr. Carolyn Ellis Staton, interim dean from 1993 to 1994. Dr. Parham Williams, dean from 1971 to 1985.

When considering the leaders of the school of law, we must not forget those who have had a strong and steady influence on the school, our faculty and staff. Chief among them are the school's emeriti law professors: Aaron Condon, Larry S. Bush, Michael Featherstone, Don L. Fruge, and Carolyn Ellis Staton. Let's recognize them. And of course we are grateful to all of our current law school faculty, and staff, and students.

This building is the first LEED, or Leadership in Energy and Environmental Design, registered building on our campus. LEED is a points rating system for high efficiency buildings. When the post-occupancy evaluation of the building is complete, we anticipate a "Gold" rating for this building.

The firm responsible for designing this stunning building is Eley & Associates of Jackson, which has won thirty-nine architectural awards, and has designed several of our beautiful and functional buildings on campus, such as our newest residential college. Jim Eley and several of his colleagues and some of their family members are here.

And the group that perfectly executed those wonderful designs is W.G. Yates & Sons Construction of Philadelphia, one of the nation's largest contractors. William G. Yates, Jr., the CEO of the firm, is an Ole Miss graduate and has also received our Engineer of Distinction Award in 1992, served on our foundation board, and is a generous financial contributor, and built our campus chapel, the Paris-Yates Chapel, among other buildings on campus.

Members of the university's own architectural and facilities planning team, Ian Banner and Chad Hunter, were an important part of the success of this building project. I also want to recognize Jeff McManus and members of the landscape services crews for making the grounds of our law center as well as our entire campus so beautiful.

This celebration is the culmination of more than seven or eight years of dedicated work by hundreds of people. The seed for this dream was planted by our former provost, Carolyn Ellis Staton, and my chief of staff, Andy Mullins. They did this over a cup of coffee, they tell me, in 2003 or 2004. They discussed the law school's need for a new home and the university's need for more classroom space.

That seed was quickly nurtured by Timothy Hall, Sam Davis, Bill Goodman, Crymes Pittman, Jamie White, Macey Edmondson, Reed Crawford, Gloria Kellum, Alice Clark, Tim Walsh, Wendell Weakley, and a host of others—many of whom are in the audience.

This dream became a reality when they and some 600 others made it their business to provide funding for our great facility. As the project evolved, dedicated law faculty and staff devoted many hours to its design. We are grateful to Kristy Gilliland and members of the committee she chaired, which helped plan and program this project. So would all our law center donors, as well as Kristy and her committee, please stand and let us say a big thank you for your support for this project.

It is now my privilege to introduce the distinguished individuals who bring greetings to us today on behalf of several groups. The first was to be our governor, the Honorable Haley Barbour, who was bringing greetings on behalf of the State of Mississippi. Regretfully, Governor Barbour had to be out-of-state today, but asked that I read this letter to you dated April 15, 2011.

### *Governor Haley R. Barbour*

Dear Chancellor Jones:

Congratulations on the dedication of the Robert C. Khayat Law Center at the University of Mississippi. This state-of-the-art facility is certainly a showpiece for the university and our state. What a special occasion it is to celebrate its opening and to honor my former professor and dear friend for whom the law center is named.

The rich history of the Ole Miss Law School, along with its innovation and growth, ensures that it will continue to be a pillar among law schools. I am proud of my Ole Miss law education and am thankful for the strong leadership and vision of Chancellor Dan Jones and Dean Richard Gershon to keep moving the University of Mississippi forward.

Marsha and I send our warmest regards and best wishes on this historic day for the university.

Sincerely,

Haley Barbour

## Chancellor Daniel W. Jones

Bringing additional greetings on behalf of our great state is Lieutenant Governor Phil Bryant. Governor Bryant was elected Mississippi's thirty-seventh lieutenant governor in 2007. His life of public service has included time as our state auditor, a member of the Mississippi House of Representatives, and as a deputy sheriff. In all his public roles, he has been a steadfast advocate for accountability in the use of public funds. We are proud that Governor Bryant's daughter, Katie Bryant, is a 2010 cum laude graduate of our law school.

Please join me in welcoming Lieutenant Governor Phil Bryant.

### *Lieutenant Governor D. Phillip Bryant*

Thank you. Good afternoon. I wish that that resume said "and a graduate of Ole Miss Law School," but I am honored that my daughter is. I tell people my happiest day in the Grove was when she graduated. This law school that we talk about both past and future has produced great men and women. Look on this stage. United States senators, judges, chief judges, world-famous authors. It will go on, I believe, as the Robert C. Khayat School of Law to produce great statesmen and public servants. Those that rise above their own interests to serve the people of the State of Mississippi and in fact, the United States of America. It has taken our children, placed them in these classrooms with fine law professors, and made out of them great jurists, great senators, great congressmen, representatives, chairmen, many are called today. But one day they were called students and generations hence will look back to this day and say again, the torch was passed.

Young attorneys will be honored to walk across the stage some day in the Grove of the Robert Khayat Law School and accept that doctor of jurisprudence. At that moment their lives will be changed. Now, for a few agonizing weeks, they will do like Katie and wait for the results of the BAR exam. Then they will go on to change the world, like Robert C. Khayat has.

Today we heard at lunch a poem that sounded more as a hymn that was written by this Renaissance man. It talked about touching the hem of the garment. A short time ago Dr. Khayat and I had an opportunity to talk, and the chancellor and I shared our faith and how we believe that the Lord has presented such opportunities to bring us here, at this moment, at this time. And I will say a prayer tonight, thankful that the Lord brought to Ole Miss and to the State of Mississippi, Robert C. Khayat. And that today we honor his service and dedicate for today, for this time, and for all time, this fine, new Robert. C. Khayat School of Law. Congratulations, Mr. Chancellor and thank you.

### CHANCELLOR DANIEL W. JONES

It is my great pleasure to now introduce Mississippi's senior U.S. Senator, the Honorable Thad Cochran. When he was on campus for the dedication of our Thad Cochran Research Center, Chancellor Khayat said that Senator Thad Cochran and the people of Mississippi have been involved in a long-term, continuous love affair. Those words are truer today than they were then, because this is Senator Cochran's thirty-ninth year on Capitol Hill.

He was elected to Congress in 1972 and elected to the U.S. Senate in 1978. Since then, he has utilized his amazing ability, his office, and his committee appointments to advocate for strong education programs around our state, and throughout our nation.

Evidence of his commitment to education and research is found at all of our state universities. Here, we owe him a great debt for advocating for our Natural Products Center, Water and Wetlands Resource Center, our Food Service Management Institute, and many other critical programs. Please welcome a great statesman, a great alumnus, and friend of the university, Senator Thad Cochran.

### *Senator W. Thad Cochran*

Thank you. Thank you very much, chancellor. I appreciate the generous introduction and especially appreciate being invited to be a part of this wonderful ceremony here today, honoring a good friend of mine, a former classmate of mine here at the University of Mississippi. We had a class in Spanish together, we got to know each other right away as students, and I came to be impressed with him, not only in the classrooms but on the fields of football and baseball, where he was All-American and really one of the finest competitors in the best sense of the word. Always a gentleman, fair, but really good. And he loved to win, and Ole Miss did win.

Well this is a special day of recognition for this new law center, honoring our friend Robert Khayat, our former chancellor, and our always loyal friend. There is no one who has done more for this university in so many different ways, and I have mentioned a few. But this law school made tremendous strides, academically and financially, under his leadership as dean and as a professor of law. The opening of the new law center will enable Ole Miss to make further contributions to the benefit of all of our state in the years to come. So I'm here to congratulate my friend Robert Khayat for this well-deserved honor and wish him much success and pleasure in the years ahead. Thank you.

### CHANCELLOR DANIEL W. JONES

We are honored to have with us today another great alumnus and friend of the university, U.S. Senator Roger Wicker. Senator Wicker was elected to the Senate in 2008, after representing us in Congress for eight terms. Senator Wicker has been a strong supporter of healthcare research. He has received the American Heart Association's National Public Service Award and the American Cancer Society's Capital Dome Award for his efforts. He has also been instrumental in bringing research funding to Mississippi universities for health-related projects that are fighting disease and improving the quality of life in our state.

Please join me in welcoming another great university friend and alumnus, Senator Roger Wicker.

*Senator Roger F. Wicker*

Thank you. Thank you, Chancellor Jones, Dr. Khayat. Ladies and gentlemen, brought to you from Moss Point High School, in cooperation with John Vaught Productions, presenting an Ole Miss adventure! His mind is faster than a speeding bullet; his drive is more powerful than a locomotive; able to leap over stubborn search committees in a single bound. Look, up in the sky box! He's a jock; he's a judge; he's a brain. Yes, he's Khayat-man! Extraordinary visitor from the other end of our state, he came to our community with strange powers and abilities far beyond those of mortal men. Khayat-man who can change the course of a mighty university, bend the will of student bodies and alumni with the force of his persuasiveness, talk elderly widows into leaving large endowments. We love you Gertrude. And who, disguised as a student athlete, Bobby Khayat, and later as a mild-mannered law professor, fights a never-ending battle for truth, justice, and the Ole Miss way.

Now, Robert, I apologize for that. But to you and your family this is a great day—for you, for Ole Miss, for the law school, and for the entire Ole Miss community. You came to Oxford in 1956, and we really never have let you go. Of course, there were brief moments practicing law, and with the Redskins, and up at Yale, but everyone always knew where you belonged and where you would end up—here and on top. For all of us, we've shared so many experiences with Robert Khayat: NCAA Foundation, NCAA probation; from the Meredith crisis to the Meredith statue crisis; from expanding the stadium to banning sticks from the stadium; from Vaught to Orgeron and everywhere in between; to Phi Beta Kappa and Croft and the Honors College; from breaking in new congressmen to breaking old stereotypes. My friends, in a way Robert Khayat has been Superman, but in a very real sense he is also every man, with the ability to be one of us—to make us see that we are all in this together. Robert, we are your family, with all the ups and downs that means, you are our man and today is your day. Congratulations.

CHANCELLOR DANIEL W. JONES

Also bringing greetings today is the Honorable William L. Waller, Jr., Chief Justice of the Supreme Court of Mississippi. Justice Waller is also an alumnus of our law school and another great friend of the university. He practiced law for more than 20 years with Waller & Waller in Jackson and was a municipal judge before being elected to the supreme court. He served as presiding justice from 2004 to 2008, and became chief justice in 2009. Please welcome the Honorable William L. Waller, Jr.

*Chief Justice William L. Waller Jr.*

It is an honor and privilege to offer a few remarks today on behalf of the judiciary. The Waller and Khayat families have been friends a long time, and I have perhaps a different view of him from what my friend, colleague, and classmate Senator Wicker offered. He and my mother used to exchange devotionals. I know him as a man of faith and a man of leadership as he served as associate dean when I was at the law school. According to Ian Banner, who has been recognized as the director of facilities and the university architect, there are three broad architectural goals in any building project: firmness, commodity, and delight. Firmness, the building must be able to fulfill its chief functions. Commodity, the building must be economical and fit for its intended use. And finally, delight, the structure should be appealing to the senses and uplifting. In my view, the Khayat Law Center went above and beyond each of these goals. In fact, I believe it is the preeminent academic structure in our state.

Why is such a building so important to the law? It is because this building communicates the vital significance of law in our society. The law brings order, structure, predictability, and a means for peaceful resolution of disputes. The Khayat Law Center symbolizes the value of law. Within these walls, students will study and engage themselves in principles, concepts, and nuances. And they will be motivated to pursue its highest ideals. Winston Churchill once said, "We shape our buildings and afterwards our buildings shape us." The beautiful state-of-the-art Khayat Center will certainly shape and inspire the future leaders of our state and nation, who in turn, will protect and advance the rule of law for generations to come. Thank you.

### CHANCELLOR DANIEL W. JONES

Also here to bring greetings on behalf of our law alumni is William C. Trotter III, known to us as "Cham." Cham is president of our Law Alumni Chapter, a group of individuals who have played a monumental role in funding this building's construction. Cham practices law with Garrard & Trotter in Belzoni. Please join me in welcoming Cham Trotter.

*William C. Trotter III*

Mr. Chief Justice, I am so delighted that I did not have to follow Senator Wicker. Ladies and gentlemen, as president of the Law Alumni Chapter of the Ole Miss Alumni Association, it is my privilege at this dedication of the Robert C. Khayat School of Law to represent the 9,684 graduates since our founding in 1854 of the Ole Miss Law School. I have been reliably informed this morning by the computer at the alumni association that at the present time—not having read the obituaries this morning—that there are 7,186 of us still alive. And I'm glad to report that a good many of us are here today to honor our friend, Robert Khayat.

This school has provided the legal education for so many distinguished lawyers, throughout not only Mississippi but well beyond our borders. And we as alumni accept the responsibility of giving back of our time, our talent, and our treasure to our alma mater. Our school of law alumni are cognizant of and we celebrate our past, we're confident in our present condition, and we're up to the challenge of the future.

You know our law school has only had five previous homes. We started in the Lyceum building in 1854 with one law school professor and seven students. In 1894 we moved just north of the Lyceum to Jefferson Hall. In 1911 Jefferson Hall was torn down to make way for the building of Peabody, and about that time the library had moved into the new library, with money from the Carnegie Foundation, which is now Bryant Hall. Well, they had that turreted building there at the beginning of the Circle; it had an "L" on the front door, so we moved into there—law school. It's now Liberal Arts. That's pretty smart. I think we do things pretty well around here. We stayed in that building until 1930, when we moved into our first new law school which was right across the Grove on the north side. It was called Lamar Hall. We stayed in there until we built a new Lamar Hall on the parking lot just east of where we had been. We renamed that building Lamar Hall, and then the old building we named after Dean Farley. We're now in Khayat Hall. You know it just sounds good to say that, doesn't it? "Hey, I'm going to class in Khayat Hall today." That's just wonderful.

You know, when we formed the Law Alumni Chapter—when the alumni association had the good sense to think about that the lawyers were ten percent of the alumni of the University of Mississippi—they were also real smart to hire a young law student as the first staff director of the Law Alumni Chapter. They paid that young law student the magnificent sum of $300 per month to do that job, and his name was Robert Khayat. Robert Khayat is our colleague; he's our professor; he's our role model; he's our chancellor; he's our sports hero; and he's always, through every bit of that, been our friend. We thank him for all he's done for our wonderful university and its law school. And our prayer is that the showers of blessing from our Heavenly Father will continue to fall upon him and his family. Thank you.

## Chancellor Daniel W. Jones

Richard Gershon became dean of the law school last July, after serving as the dean of the Charleston School of Law and the Texas Wesleyan University School of Law. Since becoming dean of our law school, Richard is already a proven leader and has demonstrated his commitment to students, faculty, and alumni. Please join me in welcoming Law Dean Richard Gershon.

### *Dean I. Richard Gershon*

Thank you, Dr. Jones. Good afternoon and thank all of you for being here on this wonderful occasion. I am pleased to represent those of us who actually get to work and teach in the building—and it is a beautiful building. It's an honor, it's a privilege to work in a building named for Chancellor Emeritus

Robert C. Khayat. As a relative newcomer, I had heard a lot about Chancellor Khayat and heard all these stories—and as Senator Wicker said—I said nobody can be that good, nobody can be Superman. He really is that good, and getting to know him has been a privilege.

We're truly grateful to everyone who made this building a reality. We're indebted to the State of Mississippi, the IHL, our U.S. senators and representatives, our outstanding university leadership for understanding the impact this building will have on education in our state, and in particular legal education in our state. We're also especially indebted to the donors, alumni, and friends of the university and the law school and of Robert Khayat who gave so generously to the campaign to make this building a reality. You built this building with your support, through your donations of time and talents. You built it with your ideas and your shared vision. You built it by not quitting when obstacles blocked your path—and when weaker or less committed people would have abandoned the effort.

We know that our challenge—those of us who work in the building, and teach there, and learn there—is to run a program of legal education worthy of this building. Our duty is to train the next generation of outstanding ethical lawyers who understand their obligation to give back to society. I can assure everyone here the faculty, staff, and students of this law school are up to that challenge. And we will fulfill our duty. Thank you.

## CHANCELLOR DANIEL W. JONES

This grand new law center provides a wonderful learning environment for our law students and our faculty. Bringing us greeting on behalf of our entire law school student body is Ms. Jaklyn Wrigley of Ocean Springs, the group's president.

Jaklyn is a member of the *Mississippi Law Journal* staff. On graduation this spring, she plans to practice law as a litigation associate with the Gulfport office of Watkins Ludlam Winter & Stennis. Please join me in welcoming Miss Jaklyn Wrigley.

*Jaklyn L. Wrigley*

Well, I'm following a bunch of tough acts, but the one welcome I would like to give is the one they cannot, and that is from the tremendous student body that I am here representing. And I think that we're the ones who really see the greatest benefit from our new law center because that's the building we live in for two and a half or three years, depending on how quickly we can go through the process. And after being in the last law center for a few years, personally, I'm very grateful for our new space. It is really just fantastic. But I hope that we can all remember that in the end it's just a building and it's really what it represents, I think, that has brought us all here today and that's the institution, the law school specifically. And it really has produced some great legal minds and I'm proud to be a part of the graduating class that will walk through those doors here in now less than a month, which is really kind of scary. And on a personal note, I was an undergraduate student here at the University of Mississippi under Chancellor Khayat, and I don't know if you know this, but we have something in common. We have two homes, here in Oxford, Mississippi, and then in Jackson County, so I'm proud to be able to make that association. But anyway, thank you for coming. I hope after this you will all come see our home and let us show you around. Thank you.

### CHANCELLOR DANIEL W. JONES

Because of the inclement weather conditions, Dr. Hank Bounds, commissioner of our Board of Trustees of State Institutions of Higher Learning, could not be with us today. In his place and stead, it is our pleasure to have Mr. Aubrey Patterson of Tupelo, a member of the Board of Trustees of the Institutions of Higher Learning. He was appointed to his post by Governor Haley Barbour. A graduate of the University of Mississippi, Michigan State University, and the University of Wisconsin, he is chairman and chief executive officer of BancorpSouth. He is a great friend of education and a wonderful friend of the University of Mississippi. He is here today on behalf of the board to present this beautiful new law center to the University of Mississippi. Please welcome Mr. Aubrey Patterson.

*Aubrey B. Patterson Jr.*

Thank you, chancellor, for that kind introduction. Commissioner Bounds does sincerely regret that he could not be here, and I'm honored to be asked to serve in his stead to present the building to the university. Thanks for allowing me to join you and thanks to also allowing you to join my good friend Dr. Stacy Davidson and his wife, they've already introduced, also serving members of the board of trustees.

We're honoring the legacy of Dr. Robert Khayat and celebrating the future of this great American public university of which this law center will be an integral part.

Dr. Khayat is already recognized by all and without a doubt one of the great education leaders of this country. And I'm honored to consider him a personal role model—and most important—a cherished friend. Since Senator Wicker has already broken the mold and given me a little latitude, I'll digress to say that he's also, besides being an acknowledged Renaissance man, a man of great judgment, when he was Colonel Rebel as a senior, he judged the university-high beauty contest and selected my wife as "most beautiful." A man of rare good judgment.

There is no doubt that his leadership has enabled this university to reach heights not dreamed possible before. And now that we know what is possible, we're encouraged to dream even bigger dreams. Knowing that they, like this law center, can come true. His legacy reaches far beyond the numbers; increases in enrollment, tremendous increases in endowment, and dramatic expansion of programs and facilities. His legacy reaches far beyond the monumental, though they are monumental accomplishments, like securing a Phi Beta Kappa chapter for the university, the Barksdale Honors College, the Croft International Institute, the Lott Leadership Institute, and garnering national recognition during the presidential debate. His legacy is yet to be fully understood but I'd be remiss if I did not also note the huge contribution his leadership has also brought to the IHL system that we serve and to the state at large. To refer to him as first among equals in that congregation of educators, understates the importance of his contribution. Due to the atmosphere his leadership created on campus and the opportunities for students that were greatly expanded during his tenure, the tens of thousands of students who matriculated here during that time will look back on their time at Ole Miss with fondness and learn to fully appreciate the role the university has played in their future successes. As a result, they'll support the university with their time and talents. They'll give back to the university and help it continue to reach new heights in the years and decades to come. Their support will ensure that future generations of Ole Miss students have even greater experiences and opportunities than they and we had.

The beautiful building we are talking about today, that we're celebrating today, represents a wonderful opportunity for the students of today and for years to come. The openness of design reflects the limitless possibilities open to the students here. It was designed not just to accommodate a certain number of students and a certain number of faculty, it was designed with the experiences and learning opportunities that students need in mind. The space allocated for the centers and clinics demonstrates that real thought was given to making attending law school at the University of Mississippi top-notch preparation for anyone planning to enter the legal field. Students can gain experience in both criminal and civil law both on the prosecutorial side and the defense side. Students can receive a law degree from here and feel confident walking into any courtroom, boardroom, or other venue of their choosing. Students who attend the Robert C. Khayat Law Center are not just attending law school, they're attending a law school that will provide them with life-changing experiences and prepare them well to succeed. Again, thank you for asking me to join you today to represent the commissioner. It's a wonderful day for Ole Miss, its students, staff, faculty, and alumni, and on behalf of the entire board of trustees I am delighted to be a part of it. Thank you.

### CHANCELLOR DANIEL W. JONES

On behalf of current and future students, faculty, and staff, Mr. Patterson, I accept this beautiful facility for the University of Mississippi. We applaud the state, federal, and private partnership that made this glorious fifty million dollar building possible.

We pledge to be good stewards of your investment. It provides a state-of-the-art learning, teaching, and research center for students, faculty, staff, and alumni.

Decade after decade, this center will enable strong legal education and research. So it is with great honor and appreciation that we acknowledge Chancellor Robert Khayat's many contributions to this university and state by naming this facility the Robert C. Khayat Law Center.

It is our hope that naming this center for Chancellor Khayat will be a permanent acknowledgement of his contributions. We wanted to make a very permanent, highly visible, and inspirational statement about his extraordinary life and transformational leadership for this university. And, we wanted to acknowledge that it was that life, and his remarkable leadership, that attracted the funding from many quarters for this exceptional building.

Now here to provide a tribute to Robert Khayat is his good friend and a good friend of the university. Since publishing *A Time to Kill* in 1988, John Grisham has written at least one novel a year, and every one of them has been an international bestseller. There are currently over 250 million John Grisham books in print world-wide in twenty-nine languages. Nine of his novels have been produced as movies, as was an original screenplay.

Who could have predicted that a young law student from Jonesboro, Arkansas, who had trouble taking Robert Khayat's essay tests, would become known as the "master of the legal thriller" and one of publishing's greatest success stories?

John and his wife, Renee, have been great friends to this university including its school of law. Programs that John and Renee have funded not only bring outstanding writers like himself to our campus each year, continue to free the wrongfully imprisoned, and enable beautiful facilities including this law center and the Grisham Library in the law center.

I have a deep appreciation for the way John and Renee have used their influence. Both in selection of topics for novels, and in the commitment of time and resources John and Renee make together, they have made a fight against injustice a priority in their lives. We're happy Renee is with us today. Renee and John are the parents of two children, Ty and Shea. Both John and Ty are graduates of our law school.

Please welcome the reigning master of the legal thriller, a graduate of our school of law, a former student of Robert Khayat, and a great friend of our university, John R. Grisham, Jr.

### *John R. Grisham Jr.*

Thank you, chancellor, for that generous introduction. I'm honored to be here today to say a few words about the law school and about Robert Khayat.

Thirty years ago, Renee and I were married on a Friday afternoon here in Oxford at the First Baptist Church. After a brief honeymoon, we were back the following Thursday for my law school graduation. The speaker that day was a retired judge, I can't recall his name, I don't recall much of what he said, but the theme of his remarks was that we were not really needed. The profession was overcrowded, too many lawyers, too many law schools. It seemed kind of an odd time and place to be dwelling on such unpleasantries. But we had heard it all before, it didn't really bother us; we had heard it for three years. We got our diplomas and we got out of here. Class of '81 was so bright and so talented we were exempted from taking the BAR exam.

When I left here thirty years ago, I did not plan to come back. I could never see myself coming back to law school. The Class of '81, as bright as we were, suffered a casualty rate in excess of fifty percent. It was a boot camp. Then it became a prolonged battle of survival and when we got out, we were done, we were gone. I could never imagine seeing or being around people like Guff Abbott, John Robin Bradley, and George Cochran, and Karen Greene, and Parham Williams, Bob Weems, and they're still there. I didn't dislike these people, but they worked for the law school and I was through with the law school. I was through forever, or so I thought.

In the fall of 1978, I walked into my first class in law school, it was Contracts, the professor was John Robin Bradley. Twenty-eight years later, my son walked into his first class in law school, it was Contracts, and the professor was John Robin Bradley. When Professor Bradley would nail a punch line, get a big laugh, my son would send me an email. And a couple of times, as I chuckled, I said "I think I've heard that before." But not all the time, there was some new material. My career as a lawyer was unremarkable and mercifully short. Nine years after we left Oxford, we were back, Renee and I, with two kids and a new profession. I was not suing people anymore, I was not practicing law, something great had happened to us, we were going a different direction, we kind of retired to Oxford to, you know, live an easier life. We were building a house then, I needed a place to write and for some reason I just gravitated back to the law school, to the library, sort of the scene of the crime. Once I got past the initial jolt, it brought back a lot of memories and as time goes by we tend to forget the bad things and remember the good ones and I kept the good memories and I actually enjoyed being up at the law school, hiding in the stacked tiers where I used to study for finals and for demanding professors, writing tales about lawyers that were not true, but certainly marketable. I'd go out in the hallway, look at the class photos and look at my class and the kids under the law school and lawyers and judges I had met along the way and even some of the law professors and I would see these professors around town, in the law school, football games, in restaurants around the Square. I was bumping into Guff Abbott, John Robin Bradley, Uncle Tommy Ethridge, some of the old guys. I liked them a whole lot more ten years later, after law school. And they were all proud of me. I got especially close to Robert Khayat.

In the fall of 1978 he was our Torts professor and our initial impression of him was somewhat guarded. He smiled a lot, he was very friendly, told jokes, and seemed genuinely concerned about our struggles during that first awful semester. And upper classmen could be heard saying things like, "Watch out. It's a setup. He smiles a lot but he'll kill you on the final exam." We were suspicious. We were suspicious. His final exam was straightforward and when he gave us good grades, our opinion of him went up tremendously. In law school certain classes bond with certain professors, and our class certainly bonded with Robert Khayat. During our second year he went off to Yale. He and Margaret packed up the kids and went to Yale for a year for reasons that were never made clear to us. I don't know what he did there. He did tell us later that nobody ever went to class at

Yale. Something significant happened though because when he left here he was Mr. Khayat, and when he came back a year later he was Dr. Khayat. He was here ten years later when we moved back, we became friends, and started a friendship that is still maturing. In 1993, the movie of *The Firm* was released and Renee and I took off to New York to a real fancy black tie premier with five thousand of our best friends that we had never met, and we had not seen the movie, and it wasn't very good, but we were able to kind of savor the moment. We came back to Oxford and said let's do this the right way. Let's have a premier here, in Oxford, at a real movie house, the Hoka. Capacity eighty-five, depending on how many chairs are broken or stolen. We sent invitations out. On the invitation the dress requirement read simply "socks optional." Khayat loved that. He framed it and hung it in his office for years. We invited a hundred friends, it was July, no air conditioning, it was hot, we served Dom Pérignon Champagne—a first for the Hoka. We weren't sure if the projectors would work for two hours nonstop, but miracles do happen. And I sat close to Robert and Margaret and we had a premier far, far finer than the one in New York. Two years later he was named chancellor and he asked me if I would say a few words at his inauguration. It was more like a coronation. Robes and pomp and ceremony and words in Latin, stuff like that. I closed my remarks that day by saying, "When I grow up, I want to be like Robert Khayat." And I'm still trying.

As chancellor, we spent even more time together, football games and fundraisers, we went to Washington to see elected officials. We had one memorable night when we honored Thad Cochran, the whole Senate was there, half of Washington was there. It was great night. It turned into a roast then it turned into a scorch. It got real ugly. It was a great night. We hosted literary functions, we hosted dinners for important people. Ole Miss was changing. New buildings were going up, new programs were being added, fundraising was setting a record, and the enrollment began this remarkable climb. He was preaching the message that this is a great public university, and people were listening. Robert Khayat showed us that we should look at the past, confront it, admit what was wrong, honor what was right, and then move on. As a natural leader, he was far more excited about the future than things that had happened in the past. He has great compassion for this state and its people. We've had long conversations about Mississippi and its problems; the lack of progress in so many areas of education, the high rates of poverty, illiteracy, high school dropout, teenage pregnancy, the cycle of poverty and drugs, and crime and prison, and how so many of our children don't really have a chance. As chancellor every year he saw hundreds of high school kids would put their money together, dreaming of college and fall short by a thousand bucks or five hundred bucks. He tirelessly raised money for these kids.

He always worried about staying too long. All successful leaders want to go out on top and he was no exception. We talked about this too much. He called me one time—Ole Miss had won a big football game—and he called me and said "I've got it all figured out. I'm leaving when Eli leaves." I said, "No, that's too soon, that's too soon." He said to me many times, he said, "You gotta tell me when I gotta go. You gotta tell when it's time to step down." And I never told him it was time to step down.

Late in his tenure we began talking about a new law school, but we first had the discussion whether or not a new law school was really needed. I suspect the old judge who spoke at my commencement was probably right. Perhaps we don't need as many corporate lawyers in tall buildings. Perhaps we don't need as many small town practitioners stacked around the Square. Maybe we don't need as many lawyers on government payrolls. But in this country, and especially in this state, today, there is a shortage of lawyers. In this country, today, at least half of our people, half of the citizens of this country, do not have access to civil justice. It's the battered wife who can't hire a lawyer for a divorce or for protection; it's the family living in a motel room because some shady bank cut corners on the foreclosure; it's the veteran denied benefits; it's the homeless child denied admission to a local school; it's the migrant worker being paid far less than minimum wage; it's the desperate family of a schizophrenic in need of a facility; it's the honest, hard-working, middle-class couple who cannot afford a lawyer to take on their insurance company. It's a long, sad list. And when you tally it all up, it covers half of us. Last year, the Gates Foundation released its The Rule of the Law Report. They looked at all wealthy, advanced nations and their population's access to civil justice. The U.S. was dead last. In Mississippi, right now, in Parchman, in the regional prisons, there are hundreds, if not thousands of innocent people locked up. Victims of a criminal justice system that is broken. They spend their days behind chain link fence, and razor wire, serving somebody else's time, and they have no lawyers. There is no one actively on the outside trying to get them out. There is no one fighting the injustice. I don't speak for this administration, I don't speak for Robert Khayat, but I hope this law school trains young lawyers, who firmly believe that a license to practice law is a powerful tool best used when defending the poor, and the weak, and the falsely accused. I don't speak for Robert Khayat, but I know him, I know he wants this law school, now so fittingly named for him, and on this campus that he cherishes, to become a driving force for social change in Mississippi. Thank you.

CHANCELLOR DANIEL W. JONES

Now, please welcome to the podium, the namesake for our new law center, Chancellor Robert C. Khayat.

*Chancellor Emeritus Robert C. Khayat*

To Chancellor Jones and his staff, my family and I thank you for what you all have done to make this day as memorable as any in our lives—as any will ever be.

To our distinguished group on the stage—we thank you for your generous comments, your humorous comments. Some of the things that you said that were close to being accurate and then some things, like Senator Wicker, that were totally accurate.

And to all of you who are here today for this event where we honor Ole Miss. Now, the Khayats are part of this and we are totally overwhelmed by it. I don't have the capability of expressing the gratitude that we feel to the university and to the people of Ole Miss for your kindness to us through the years. Margaret Khayat and I, our children Margaret and Robert Jr., have always felt loved and nurtured, embraced, and protected by the University of Mississippi. Even when the person from Missoula, Montana wrote me and told me that he was going to kill me for destroying the culture of the South by banning sticks from the football stadium at Ole Miss. We knew he loved us in spite of that.

John and Renee Grisham have been kind to Margaret and me since our first meeting. Today, we thank John for the generous introduction, and for the thoughtful introduction regarding the role of law, and we thank the Grisham family for enabling us—us being the university—to build this wonderful law center.

Fifty-five years ago, June 2, 1956, my brother Eddie, who is here, drove me from our home in Moss Point to Oxford on a Saturday, dropped me at Garland Dormitory, and said, "Stay off the road to Memphis." And I heard him. I listened.

I was anxious. I was uncertain. I was lonely. I was homesick, and I began to try to grasp life at Ole Miss.

Those of us who were here in those years, those wonderful idyllic years between World War II and some of the events that happened later—that were difficult for all of us—were taught and inspired by gifted faculty, who expected and demanded our best in their classrooms. That experience in the classrooms with the faculty was enriched and expanded by participation in student life—in my case in athletics—and by establishing relationships and friendships with students, staff, and faculty that have lasted a lifetime. Seeds of affection and respect were planted lovingly and nurtured by the staff who looked after us—the people who helped us register for classes, take the courses we needed, or counseled us in so many ways.

I might tell you that one of my counseling responsibilities early in my chancellorship came from a young man named John Joseph from Montgomery, who later became president of the student body and a Truman scholar, who came in to see me.

We sat on the sofa and I said, "What can I do for you John?"

He said, "I have a question."

"Let's hear it."

"What do you do with girls?"

I said, "What did you say John?"

He said, "What do you do with girls?"

I said, "What do you mean 'what do you do with girls?'"

He said, "Well I've never been with a girl. What do I do? Do I hold hands? Or do I put my arm around her? Or what do I do?"

I thought I knew that I was called to intellectual challenges as leader of a university of this quality. I just told John to depend on the young women to help him along and that things would work out. And they did. He is happily married. He and his wife have a daughter named Anna. He is successful. They live in Montgomery and like so many other Ole Miss students, including many of you, John stays in touch with us—people in our office.

The people who counseled us, and helped us, really were our fathers and mothers at Ole Miss. There were also those who provided food, housing, health care, and general support. We often joked that if we could bathe, dress, and feed ourselves, the faculty and staff would take care of all our other needs. That's all we had to do. Bathing was sometimes a challenge. In truth, these people enabled us to enjoy our college experience to the fullest, and they sparked an affection for Ole Miss that could not be diminished.

My friend, classmate, and the leader of our football teams—Charlie Flowers—has labeled our years at Ole Miss as "Camelot." Our friendships and our affection for the school have been enriched through the years, and many of you in this audience have helped the university, have helped this chancellor and other chancellors—including the current chancellor—and you've helped our family. The University of Mississippi and the Khayats are profoundly grateful.

As I thought about appropriate remarks for this dedication, I realized I could not limit my comments to the law school. That's because the beautiful law school building, the grounds, and the important teaching and learning that will take place in that building represent the mission, the personality, and the character of our entire university.

We began the journey in 1848; the Lyceum doors first opened. Six years later, we became the fourth public law school in America. For 154 years, thousands of lawyers and leaders have been educated and trained in our law school. Most of those graduates have made remarkable contributions to our society at the local level as stalwarts in their communities, as leaders in government, and in their personal lives.

You look across this stage, and you see lawyers. Not everyone up here is a lawyer, but people who are in government, in top leadership positions, a minister, an educator or two. People who care very deeply about our country, about this university, and about the role of law. We have among us America's foremost writer. There are people in all walks of life who hold law degrees from our law school who have made a difference, and that includes my previously mentioned friend Charlie Flowers.

When you visit the building you are going to see it's beautiful, it is functional, it is state-of-the-art, and it was built by Yates Construction Company. Bill Yates, who took a small company in Philadelphia, Mississippi and developed it into one of the great construction companies in America, is a graduate of the Ole Miss law school.

I think the new building is tangible proof of the commitment our university has made to teaching, to learning, and to function and to beauty, and to leadership. Jim Eley was our architect. He and his team used the latest design techniques and they created plans for a distinguished structure that will operate efficiently. It will serve the needs of our faculty and staff, and students, and our visitors who come to our campus. You will find the building to be not only stunning, but an extremely well-built, modern law building.

In addition to meeting the traditional expectations of a building, this law building provides an attractive and stunning welcome to our campus. The beauty of the Ole Miss campus is one of our strengths. The years that all of us have loved and nurtured this place we have seen it become more beautiful—to reach a point where it makes a strong impact on people who come to see us just by what they see on the campus and of course that is reinforced by the warmth they feel from the people.

Law Professor and Provost Carolyn Staton initiated this project. She felt we needed a new law building and she knew we needed more classrooms—our enrollment had increased dramatically. She was relentless in pursuit of both building a new law building and having additional classrooms. She pushed and she prodded a lot of people to help, and she did not rest until the decision was made that we would build a state-of-the-art, wonderful law school building. Carolyn Staton, our provost and the person who really had the original idea for this building, please stand and allow us to recognize you.

During my years as chancellor, probably because of my life on teams, we operated as a team. As you know, many people are involved in planning and constructing a fifty million dollar law center. We sought support from the legislature, and thankfully we received a positive response. We sought assistance from the federal government, and thankfully again we received support. But the bulk of the funding for this facility, as is the case with most Ole Miss buildings, had to come from the private sector.

More than 600 donors participated in a law school campaign, thus far contributing more than thirty-seven million dollars to the total cost of the facility. I believe that Dr. Jones this week was able to reach agreement with another donor at a major level that will probably help us finish out the amount that we need to have all the funds needed to pay for the building.

We had, as we always do at Ole Miss, a group of volunteers who led the way for us. One of the chairs of that committee was Bill Goodman and I know he is here, and Crymes Pittman was a chair, and I don't know if Crymes is here or not. Bill Goodman and Crymes Pittman will you please stand.

They and the members of the committee led the way. They had the strong guidance of a member of our management team. I am going to ask several members of our management team to stand and be recognized as a group. During my years as chancellor we tried to divide up responsibility and let different members of the team lead. In this particular case we were going to build a law building. Although everybody was committed to it, there were several people who had specific responsibilities. One was Gloria Kellum, she led the development area. Then Larry Sparks, who is our chief financial officer, had to find a way to manage the resources that we had, to be able to move forward with the project, utilize state funds, federal funds, and private support, and self-generated funds. Andy Mullins who worked closely with the legislature to see that that legislation was passed. Ian Banner, our university director of campus facilities and planning worked closely with the architects and the builders. And Jeff McManus, our incredibly gifted director of landscape services, are the people from our staff who worked most closely with the development of the law building. I would ask you to please express your appreciation to them because they deserve it.

From the moment the dream of this new law center was born and began, the words of Isaiah 40: 30–31 were in my mind and in my heart and constantly in front of me. And they are familiar words, and I suspect that you will recognize them. I saw them as being applicable not only to the law school project but to our university, to our state, and to our nation. The familiar words from Isaiah: "Even the youths shall faint and be weary, and the young men shall utterly fall. But they that wait upon the Lord shall renew their strength. They shall mount up with wings like Eagles; they shall run, and not be weary; and they shall walk and not faint."

Again and again and again we have watched the people of Ole Miss rise like eagles to accomplish the impossible. Our people—our faculty, students, staff, alumni, and friends—never weary of their efforts to make this university better, and they never faint when Ole Miss calls. It is this spirit that has enriched our lives in countless ways.

I thank you, the people of Ole Miss, first for the opportunity of having spent a lifetime here, including serving as chancellor, and for the rich and rewarding life that you have given to me and to my family. But more than that I thank you for your devotion to this university, for your spirit, and for your friendship. Thank you.

### CHANCELLOR DANIEL W. JONES

Thank you, chancellor. In a moment I will ask you to stand again and join in the singing of our Alma Mater, which will be led by Miss Briana Logan Raif, a second-year law student and Ole Miss Bachelor of Music and Vocal Performance graduate. You will find the words of the Alma Mater in your program. I will ask you to remain standing for our benediction, which will be delivered by Dr. Morris Stocks—our provost, vice chancellor for academic affairs, and professor of Accountancy. Following the benediction, I will ask that you please join us over in the Robert C. Khayat Law Center's lobby for a reception and open house.

### *Provost Morris H. Stocks*

Please join with me in prayer. Most gracious Heavenly Father, we come to you this afternoon with grateful hearts. Hearts full of thanksgiving for your grace, for your love, for your immeasurable blessings. We thank you for those who are gathered to share in this wonderful occasion. We thank you Father for the dedicated men and women who have worked to make our magnificent law center a reality. From the inspiration of our gifted leaders, to those who organized and planned, to alumni and friends who gave freely of their time and resources, to those who labored to raise the beautiful structure. May they have a sense of delight in their accomplishment and recognize that lives have been changed forever because of their investment.

We thank you, Father, for Chancellor Robert Khayat, for the influence he's had on each of us. We thank you for his leadership, his vision, and his life committed to self-less service. We thank you for the tremendous impact that he has had on our university and our state. We pray that your anointing will rest upon him and his family. We give thanks for the faculty, staff, and leadership of the school of law. We ask that you guide the faculty, help them to impart knowledge, encourage them to inspire, and to bring truth and understanding to those they teach. We pray for guidance for the leadership of the school of law as they work to serve mankind and make life better for all. We pray that the Robert C. Khayat Law Center will be a thriving spirited home of inspired discovery and sound learning. Guide our students as they embark on the exciting path before them. Give them wisdom, vision, and courage. We celebrate the dedication of the Robert C. Khayat Law Center. Bless all who grace her halls, grant a spirit of community and an atmosphere of hope for all who are a part of this special place. We ask all this in your holy name. Amen.

*Chancellor Jones, Chancellor Emeritus Khayat, and John Grisham enjoy the dedication ceremony

*Chancellor Emeritus Khayat addresses the audience at the dedication ceremony

*On Monday, October 2, 1854, the Lyceum building hosted William Forbes Stearns' first class meeting of the department of law at the University of Mississippi

*Ventress Hall housed the school of law from 1911 to 1930

*From 1930 to 1978, Lamar Hall served as the home of the school of law. Renamed Farley Hall, the Meek School of Journalism and New Media is now located in this building

*In the summer of 1978, the school of law moved into the newly constructed Lamar Law Center, where it remained until 2011

*The formal plans for the building that would become the Robert C. Khayat Law Center were completed on February 29, 2008

*In January 2011, classes began in the state-of-the-art Robert C. Khayat Law Center

*Following the dedication ceremony, alumni and friends gathered in the new law center for a reception

*Chancellor Emeritus Khayat enjoys the reception in the atrium of the Robert C. Khayat Law Center

# TRIBUTES TO CHANCELLOR EMERITUS ROBERT C. KHAYAT

### Dean I. Richard Gershon*

April 15, 2011, was a historic day for the law school, the university, and the State of Mississippi. Alumni, faculty, students, and friends of the law school from throughout the country gathered in Oxford, MS to celebrate the dedication of the law school's new building to one of our most distinguished graduates: Robert C. Khayat. Despite the threat of inclement weather, the day's events were a success. The ceremony was moved from the grounds of the new law center to the Gertrude C. Ford Performing Arts Center. There, a group of distinguished alumni, including John Grisham, honored Robert Khayat's service to the university and challenged current and future students to live up to the noble profession to which they have been called. Following the ceremony, guests attended a reception in the new law center, where student leaders led them on tours of the building. Visitors could not help but be impressed by its magnificence and beauty. Indeed, those of us who are fortunate to work and learn in this building appreciate the generous support of the donors who made this vision a reality. We are proud to call this new building home.

This state-of-the-art, LEED certified building will help us enhance the strong reputation of our law school. It has already hosted the United States Environmental Justice and the Law Symposium, sponsored by the American Bar Association, and we are confident that it will attract many programs of national and even global importance. The Robert C. Khayat Law Center will

---

\* Dean and professor of law, University of Mississippi. Prior to joining the University of Mississippi School of Law, Dean Gershon served as the founding dean of the Charleston School of Law and the dean of Texas Wesleyan University School of Law in Fort Worth, Texas. Dean Gershon was also on the faculty at Stetson University School of Law from 1984 to 1998. He is a graduate of the University of Georgia (B.A. 1979), the University of Tennessee (J.D. 1982), and the University of Florida (LL.M. Taxation 1983). He is the author of several books and articles on taxation and legal education. Dean Gershon serves on the Mississippi Access to Justice Commission, The Mississippi Bar Professionalism Committee, and the Boys and Girls Clubs Advisory Board.

provide the law school with the technological capability to allow our students here in Oxford to connect with judges and lawyers everywhere in our state and region. It will also provide the law school the possibility to create advanced degree programs reaching students in all parts of the world through distance learning. In fact, in the short time that we have been in the new building, we have already taken substantial steps forward. The law school faculty has recently approved an innovative new skills program that will enhance the way our students are prepared for entry into the legal profession, and it has also voted to take the initial steps in creating a new LL.M. program.

We recognize, however, that as impressive as this building is, and as many opportunities as it will provide our students, it alone does not make this law school great. It is the people, and the programs they create, that define its character. This is one of the many lessons we can learn from Chancellor Emeritus Robert Khayat, who above all, invested in the University of Mississippi family. This new building, along with Chancellor Khayat's example, challenges each of us—alumni, faculty, staff, and students—to devote new energy to carry the law school to new heights. And we will rise to that challenge. We will continue to devote our time and resource to our students, providing them with an outstanding professional education and training them to be ethical lawyers who understand the importance of service to their local communities. We will continue to have an ever growing impact on the legal profession and legal education both in our state and beyond. If our efforts match the excellence of our new building and even approximate the devotion of the man whose name it bears, then there is no doubt we will accomplish that goal.

It is a great time to be a part of the University of Mississippi School of Law. Our future is very bright.

## GOVERNOR WILLIAM F. WINTER*

On the historic and hauntingly beautiful campus of Ole Miss, we are reminded on every hand of a legion of extraordinary men and women who have played a visionary and defining role in the sustaining of the university over more than 160 years. Through good times and bad, through wars and depressions, through civil and political strife, they have provided the faith and stability to overcome the nay-sayers and the mindless critics of progress that seem to be a part of every generation.

We see the names of these heroes gracing many of the imposing buildings that give an aura of strength and permanence to this historic school. It is obviously impossible in this space to note all of the names that appear on those buildings—names like Barnard and Lamar,[1] Fulton and Bondurant,[2] Hume and

---

\* William F. Winter is a shareholder at the Jackson-based firm, Watkins Ludlam Winter & Stennis, P.A. Prior to joining the firm, Mr. Winter served the State of Mississippi as Governor (1980-1984), Lt. Governor (1972-1976), Mississippi State Treasurer (1964-1968), Mississippi State Tax Collector (1956-1964), and Representative in the Mississippi House of Representatives (1948-1956). Recognized by President Bill Clinton as "a great champion of civil rights," William Winter's gubernatorial tenure is most well-known for its leadership in encouraging equal opportunities in publicly-funded primary education regardless of race or class.

Born in Grenada, Mississippi, in 1923, William Winter served in the armed forces in both World War II and the Korean War. He received a B.A. from the University of Mississippi in 1943 and an LL.B. in 1949. While in law school, Mr. Winter served as the Editor-In-Chief of the *Mississippi Law Journal*.

In addition to a distinguished political career, Mr. Winter has received numerous professional honors, distinctions, and honorary degrees. President Clinton appointed Mr. Winter to the National Advisory Board on Race Relations in June 1997. He is also the recipient of the John F. Kennedy Profile in Courage Award and a fellow of the Mississippi Bar Association.

In 1999, Mr. Winter helped found the William Winter Institute for Racial Reconciliation, whose mission is to build more inclusive communities by promoting diversity and citizenship, and by supporting projects that help communities solve local challenges.

[1] Frederick A.P. Barnard was the university's first chancellor from 1856 to 1861. The Center for the Study of Southern Culture is housed in Barnard Observatory.
L.Q.C. Lamar was a university faculty member and director of the Law Department until 1870, the year Mississippi was readmitted into the Union. In 1888, Lamar was appointed to the United States Supreme Court, the only Mississippian to date to hold that distinction. The law school resided in Lamar Hall prior to its new home in the Robert C. Khayat Law Center.

[2] Robert B. Fulton served as chancellor from 1892 to 1906 and is credited with establishing the school of engineering, school of education, and school of medicine.

Farley[3]—to reference only a few. They laid the foundation for the university's present-day eminence.

Now we add another name to that pantheon of heroes, as we dedicate the magnificent building, which bears the name of one of its most illustrious graduates—Robert C. Khayat.

It is fitting that this building should be named for him. Distinguished alumnus, outstanding teacher and administrator for many years, nationally heralded chancellor, Robert Khayat lends stature and prestige to the University of Mississippi. No one in its long history has been more meaningfully involved in the affairs of the university in so many transforming ways.

From his school years at Moss Point High School, where he was a student-leader and stellar athlete, Robert showed the special qualities that foreshadowed his later achievements. It was not just by random chance that he had those successes. He owes much to his wise and loving parents, Eddie and Eva Khayat, who infused him with the values and sense of purpose that set him apart. Their entire family, including a brother and two sisters, reinforced and encouraged each other.

Robert learned what it was to compete academically and athletically not just in high school but at Ole Miss where he starred in both football and baseball and earned Hall of Fame honors as a student. He was a standout member of the fabled 1959 football team, arguably the best in school history. He was selected to the National Football League Pro-Bowl Team during his tenure there.

Not content with his achievements as a premier professional athlete and all of the public acclaim that accompanies such a career, he began to respond to the calling of the profession that

---

During Fulton's tenure, football was introduced to the school as was the school's first printed annual, *The Ole Miss*.

Alexander Lee Bondurant was the first dean of the graduate school from 1927 to 1936 as well as acting chancellor in 1921. Bondurant also established and coached the first football team in 1893.

[3] Alfred Hume served two terms as chancellor from 1924 to 1930, and then from 1932 to 1935. Hume is credited with preventing Governor Theodore G. Bilbo from moving the university to Jackson.

Robert J. Farley served as dean of the law school from 1947 to 1963 and president of the Mississippi Bar from 1954 to 1955. Before moving to Lamar Hall, the law school resided in Farley Hall.

was his first love and his life-long passion. While still playing pro football with the Washington Redskins, he enrolled in the Ole Miss School of Law. Upon graduation he began a thriving career as a lawyer in his home county for several years, but then Ole Miss beckoned to him again—this time as a member of its faculty. It was a fortuitous coming together—the confluence of a proud alumnus with his beloved alma mater and a successful lawyer with the dedicated teacher of the law.

Here he became an exemplary model for his students, teaching them far more than the complex intricacies of the law, as he shared with them the practical wisdom that came from his own fascinating life experiences. At a time when Mississippi was emerging from its self-imposed social and cultural isolation, Robert Khayat, with a vision of a more open and less insular society, played a major role in the enlightenment of an entire generation of young law students. He helped develop in them an enhanced appreciation for the majesty of the law and their duty as lawyers to defend our legal and political system against the mindless critics who would profane and diminish it.

As his former students began to fill positions of leadership in the profession and in political and civic affairs, his unique influence started to be felt across the state in the emergence of a more progressive atmosphere that challenged some of the old provincial shibboleths based on race and gender. While there were many other enlightened members of our profession who helped drive this change, the strong and respected voice of Robert Khayat was a particularly effective force.

Because he had emerged in a non-confrontational way as an influential advocate for sensible and progressive ideas, he became the obvious choice to lead the university when Chancellor Gerald Turner resigned to become the president of Southern Methodist University in 1994.[4] Robert Khayat was unanimously elected chancellor by the Mississippi Board of Trustees of State Institutions of Higher Learning.

By any measure, it will be recorded that in the fifteen years under his dynamic leadership Ole Miss progressed more

---

[4] Robert Gerald Turner was the second youngest chancellor in the university's history, serving from 1984 to 1995. During Turner's tenure, the university's endowment grew from $8 million to $64 million.

dramatically than in any comparable period in its history. That progress includes growth in the number and quality of its students and faculty; in its financial support and endowment; in its incredibly lovely pristine campus; in the buildings, laboratories, and library; in the art, music, and athletic facilities; in its greatly expanded areas of service to the state and nation; and most impressively, in its national standing and prestige.

When Robert became chancellor, he set as his goal the achieving for Ole Miss national recognition as one of America's great public universities. There are many unbiased observers who feel that he achieved that objective. What is universally agreed on is that Dr. Khayat, in his distinguished tenure as chancellor, set a standard for leadership that stamps him as one of Mississippi's all-time greatest transformational figures.

In his preface to Dr. Allen Cabaniss's 1948 *Centennial History of the University of Mississippi,* Ole Miss alumnus Dr. Peter Kyle McCarter, professor of English and dean of the university, wrote these words:

> Following tradition and sentiment, which all of us love if we are worthy of our humanity, we sing and speak of *Alma Mater.* And what is "Ole Miss" but *Alma Mater* rendered into our more congenial Southern speech? Yet could there not be another symbolic figure for a great institution of learning and public service, the figure of a man in his prime years, a man with the deep brow of a scholar, the keen eye of the observer and seeker, the strong body that bespeaks the life of action, the capability of endurance, and the power to fight, if need be; a man who, let us say, has learned to live, as great men do live, by faith and reason reconciled; and one who can never be content with his own horizons or complacent about his own limitations? And may not such a figure symbolize, God willing, the University of Mississippi?

Do not those words also describe Chancellor Emeritus Robert C. Khayat?

## Dr. Daniel P. Jordan[*]

In the halcyon days of the 1950s at Ole Miss, Vardaman Dormitory was home to a special group of scholarship athletes. Vardaman A was reserved for the freshmen football squad and Vardaman B for the baseball and basketball teams. Meanwhile, the varsity football players lived in palatial luxury in Garland. The upperclassmen went to great lengths to provide a warm welcome for the rookies. "Freshmen Meetings" were less about academic subjects than giving the varsity of all sports a chance to improve their baseball swings while toughening up the posteriors of the frosh for the competition ahead.

In September 1956, Robert Khayat of 520 Beardslee Street in Moss Point, and myself of 1 Shady Lane, Philadelphia, arrived at Vardaman. Robert was destined to be a star in both football and baseball. I learned to look at life very philosophically as a subpar athlete in basketball and baseball. We also shared a common faith as well as membership in the famous "Freshmen Class" at the University Methodist Church. Our iconic teacher and mentor was Dean Emeritus of Men Malcolm Guess,[5] and his sophomore assistant was Mary Ann Mobley,[6] a future Miss America.

---

[*] Dr. Jordan was a scholarship letterman in basketball and baseball, served as student body president, and has been elected to both the student and alumni Halls of Fame at Ole Miss. He holds a Ph.D. in American history from the University of Virginia where he was elected to Phi Beta Kappa and was later a scholar in residence. From 1985 to 2008, he served as president of the Thomas Jefferson Foundation (Monticello). Lou Jordan is a former Miss Ole Miss. The Jordans have three children, now all adults, including the Honorable Daniel P. Jordan III, an Ole Miss graduate with distinction and a federal district judge with chambers in Jackson, Mississippi. For assistance with this essay, Dr. Jordan wishes to thank Lou Jordan, Warner and Kay Alford, and Sue Keiser.

[5] R. Malcolm Guess attended the University of Mississippi as a student from 1908 to 1913. In 1922, Guess was hired by the university to serve as general secretary of the YMCA. He was later appointed dean of men in addition to serving as YMCA secretary in 1933. Dean Guess ended his role as secretary in 1947 to serve as dean of men full-time. Guess retired from his position with the university in 1955. *Finding Aid for the R. Malcolm Guess Collection*, UNIV. OF MISS. LIBRARIES: ARCHIVES AND SPECIAL COLLECTIONS (last visited Aug. 1, 2011), http://www.olemiss.edu/depts/general_library/archives/finding_aids/MUM00566.html.

[6] Mary Ann Mobley Collins graduated from the University of Mississippi in 1958. Also in 1958, Ms. Mobley was crowned Miss Mississippi followed by her Miss America win in 1959. Ms. Mobley went on to star in two films with Elvis Presley in 1965 and countless other films and television appearances throughout her forty-year long career. Ms. Mobley has been married to actor Gary Collins since 1967 and the couple has one

Attendance was excellent. Over time, Robert and I also developed a keen interest in the Chi Omega Sorority. Fortune smiled there in leading us to our wives of now almost fifty years, Margaret Denton (now Khayat) and Lou Schmelzer (now Jordan).[7]

Robert and I majored in history and came under the spell of such marvelous professors as John Hebron Moore,[8] and his wife Margaret, and the controversial and courageous James W. Silver.[9] In our spare time, we marched as "ground pounders" in the Army R.O.T.C. Along the way I came to know Robert extremely well and to admire him enormously. Our friendship would be close and lifelong. And I was far from alone because Robert's capacity for friendship was—and is—limitless.

It was a fabulous time to be at Ole Miss. Robert and others have called it a Rebel Camelot. And why not?—the Korean War had ended in an armistice, and the Vietnam War hadn't begun. Also ahead were the turbulent 1960s and 70s which rocked America with terrible assassinations, violent protests, and national discord. In our comfortable and lovely cocoon in Oxford, Ole Miss seemed invincible and the place to be. The football team won two national championships (among other distinctions), and the baseball team, our junior and senior years, captured the SEC title only to be denied by state segregation policies two trips to Omaha for the College World Series. We also reveled in back-to-

---

adult daughter. *See* THE OFFICIAL WEBSITE OF MARY ANN MOBLEY: BIOGRAPHY, www.maryannmobley.net/?page_id=32 (last visited Aug. 1, 2011); *Miss America crowns University Libraries a top priority*, 2 THE UNIVERSITY OF MISSISSIPPI J.D. WILLIAMS LIBRARY: KEYWORDS 11 (Spring 2008).

[7] To extend the story, Robert's roommate was Warner Alford, who married Coach Swayze's daughter Kay, an Ole Miss beauty and brain and Lou's big sister in the sorority.

[8] A native Mississippian, John Hebron Moore and his wife Margaret Deschamps Moore both served as history professors at the University of Mississippi. John Moore wrote multiple books analyzing the South, particularly agriculture in Mississippi. John Moore retired from the history department at Florida State University in 1993. *New Books for Spring / Summer 2010*, THE UNIV. OF S.C. PRESS 21 (2010), http://www.sc.edu/uscpress/catalogs/SS10.pdf.

[9] James Wesley Silver was an American History professor at the University of Mississippi from 1936 to 1964. Silver later taught at Notre Dame University and the University of South Florida before retiring in 1982. Alan Krebs, *James W. Silver, 81, a Professor Who Fought for Racial Equality*, N.Y. TIMES (July 26, 1988), at B7.

back Miss Americas,[10] several Rhodes Scholars,[11] a stunningly beautiful campus (especially in the spring), and the general belief that we were hot stuff and destined for big things. It's fair to say we were self-confident if not cocky. Of course, we were largely oblivious to the terrible realities of racism and Mississippi's widespread poverty. That illusion was shattered in the fall of 1962 and the turmoil around the arrival of James Meredith. It is my belief that Robert's inspired and enlightened leadership as chancellor moved Ole Miss beyond its ugly past in race relations into a bright new era of robust diversity and progress. He also restored a previous joy, optimism, and self-esteem among the student body, faculty, alumni, and friends of the university. Robert transformed all aspects of the school—but his lasting contribution might be intangible in the re-establishment of the true Ole Miss spirit based on more substantive pride than beauty contests and brawn.

Athletics had a powerful influence on Robert, an influence that would later help him become the greatest chancellor in the history of the University of Mississippi. This argument can be overstated, but consider the positions he played. In football, he set records as a place kicker—a solitary role in the spotlight when, at times, the game was on the line.[12] He also played in the middle of the line—an excellent school of humility (and who is more modest and self-effacing than Robert?) where one's manhood, wile, and tenacity were routinely tested. In baseball, he earned accolades as a catcher—the quarterback of the team. And speaking of teams, in both sports Robert exemplified the attributes of a successful athlete. He was self-sacrificing; he had passion for the game; he understood the necessity of determination, loyalty, careful planning, and playing smart, as well as hard; and he had the sine

---

[10] Mary Ann Mobley's win in 1959 was followed by Lynda Lee Mead (now Shea) earning the Miss America title in 1960. Both were members of the Chi Omega Sorority while attending Ole Miss. *People*, TIME MAGAZINE (Sept. 21, 1959), at 49.

[11] Twenty-five students from the University of Mississippi have earned the Rhodes Scholarship. HISTORY: THE UNIVERSITY OF MISSISSIPPI, http://www.olemiss.edu/info/history.html (last visited Aug. 1, 2011).

[12] Khayat led the nation in scoring by a kicker in both 1958 and 1959. To date, he is the only player in Ole Miss history to achieve that feat in consecutive seasons. Barbara Lago, *Chancellor Announces Retirement Plans*, OLE MISS SPORTS (last visited Aug. 1, 2011), http://www.olemisssports.com/genrel/010609aaa.html.

qua non of being a leader. He also lived by the Bear Bryant rule: "If we win, they did it. If we tie, we did it. If we lose, I did it." Robert is without equal in deflecting, to others, credit which rightly should be given to Robert himself.

Robert has acknowledged his debt to the talented staff of the football team. I also know of his immense admiration for Coach Thomas King Swayze, Ole Miss's chief recruiter and legendary coach of the baseball team.[13] Coach Swayze was a ferocious competitor who had mastered the game of baseball. Perhaps more importantly, he had an eye for talent, knew how to build a team, made the game fun, and was unparalleled as a motivator.[14] It's no accident—in my view—that this profile sounds like Chancellor Khayat. I have often said, before audiences at Ole Miss and elsewhere, that the most important lessons I know about management, I learned from Coach Swayze. I'm sure Robert would agree.

People are rightly captivated by Robert's personality which is warm, transparent, upbeat, and considerate. His intellectual capacity is shown in his being an Academic All-American as well as his finishing third in his class in law school, and his having earned a masters of law from Yale. Perhaps more important is Robert's emotional IQ. One cannot find a more empathic individual or one who is more kind and caring or who has a greater gift of friendship more deeply rooted in sincerity and understanding. All of the above was clear on the baseball diamond.

Let me attempt to summarize a lot in one vignette. In our sophomore year, the baseball team was young and finding its way. Late in the season, we had a critical home series against our arch-rival, Alabama. The score was tied when I entered the game under daunting circumstances as a relief pitcher. I survived the jam,

---

[13] Coach Thomas K. (Tom) Swayze was a three-year letterman in football and a four-year letterman in baseball as a student-athlete at the University of Mississippi before coaching the Ole Miss Rebels baseball team from 1951 to 1971. During his tenure Coach Swayze amassed a record of 361-201-2 which includes three appearances in the College World Series. *See Ole Miss Legend Tom Swayze Passes Away at 93*, OLE MISS SPORTS (Feb. 1, 2003), http://www.olemisssports.com/sports/m-basebl/spec-rel/020103aaa.html.

[14] Coach Tom Swayze is commonly referred to as the first recruiting coordinator in the South. *Id.*

pitched several hitless innings, and got the win. Robert, as our catcher, inspired confidence by making the right calls and always providing a big target. In the locker room afterwards, Robert came over, said "here's a souvenir for you," and tossed me the game ball. My office has always been devoid of vanity space, but it has also had, on a shelf, a solitary now-yellowed baseball on which is written: "Ole Miss 6, Alabama 5." Robert Khayat has enriched the lives of countless individuals with his quiet and thoughtful acts of kindness.

All who were student-athletes with Robert knew that he was destined for greatness. None of us was surprised in the least at his transcendent success as chancellor. We will always be deeply grateful for his unparalleled contributions to our alma mater and to our state and nation—and especially for his loyal and generous friendship across the years.

## Charlie Flowers[*]

It is a great honor to write a few words about my old teammate and dear friend of fifty years. I find it impossible to write about him without the use of superlatives. I do not apologize for this for the simple reason that Robert happens to be the finest person I have ever known. Robert came to Ole Miss with the freshman class of 1956—possibly the greatest class both athletically as well as academically in the history of the university. In addition to their remarkable success on the football field,[15] Robert's class went on to produce several pro-football players, several lawyers and doctors, an Ole Miss athletic director, an Ole Miss head baseball coach, and a number of college coaches and high school educators. Also in that freshman class was Robert's great friend Warner Alford.[16] Little did they know at the time that they would spend the greater part of their lives working to make Ole Miss a better place. They have certainly succeeded in that endeavor.

One of the first things I noticed about Robert when he arrived on campus was how, through no apparent effort on his part, everyone simply gravitated to him, especially the football players. And believe me, considering the different individuals on that team

---

[*] Charlie Flowers is a member of the College Football Hall of Fame and served as the captain of the 1959 National Champion Ole Miss football team. Originally from Marianna, Arkansas, Flowers started at fullback from 1957 to 1959 and earned All-America honors both athletically and academically during that time. Following his tenure at Ole Miss, Flowers went on to play in the NFL for franchises in Los Angeles, San Diego, and New York. Flowers has been inducted into the Mississippi Sports Hall of Fame and the Ole Miss Athletic Hall of Fame, is a member of the Ole Miss Team of the Century, and is still the record holder of the highest rushing average per play in a season with 7.4 yards. COLLEGE FOOTBALL HALL OF FAME, http://www.collegefootball.org/famer_selected.php?id=50101 (last visited Aug. 1, 2011); Ole Miss Histories and Records, CBS SPORTS COLLEGE NETWORK, http://grfx.cstv.com/photos/schools/ole/genrel/auto_pdf/all-time-results-0810.pdf (last visited Aug. 1, 2011).

[15] From 1956 to 1959, the Ole Miss Rebels football team amassed a record of 35-7-1. Ole Miss Histories and Records, CBS SPORTS COLLEGE NETWORK, http://grfx.cstv.com/photos/schools/ole/genrel/auto_pdf/all-time-results-0810.pdf (last visited Aug. 1, 2011).

[16] Warner Alford served as Ole Miss athletic director from 1978 to 1994, and later held the position of executive director of the University of Mississippi Alumni Association. OLE MISS ALUMNI ASSOCIATION, http://olemissalumni.com/news/default.aspx?page_id=330 (last visited Aug. 1, 2011).

that was no small feat. Even then Robert displayed the defining characteristic that no doubt made him so admired—to put it simply—it was impossible not to want him as your friend. This characteristic was on display when he was asked to run for Colonel Rebel in his senior year.[17] Wanting to support Robert, the entire football team campaigned on his behalf. Because the team was somewhat isolated from the rest of the students—players were required to sleep in the same dorm and eat in the same dining hall—some wondered if Robert had enough on-campus exposure to win. However, we quickly found that the team's isolation did not hurt Robert's chances at all. In fact, it was impossible to find anyone who wasn't going to vote for him. Obviously, he won in a land slide!

Another thing I immediately noticed about Robert was his innate toughness. Robert played tackle on both offense and defense for four years during his time at Ole Miss, and one thing's for certain: no one could play that position under Coach John Vaught without being tough. But when I think of Robert's football career at Ole Miss, I am reminded not only of his physical toughness but his mental toughness as well. During the 1959 season, on a freezing November day in Memphis, we played the University of Tennessee. The previous week, Tennessee had knocked LSU out of the unbeaten ranks, which made our game even more important. With a record of 7-1 we knew a win would send us to a major bowl game. For the first half it was an extremely hard-fought game. With just seconds to go before halftime, Robert came into the game and kicked a frozen football 47 yards against the wind right between the goal posts, and we entered the locker room leading 10-7. You never saw a more fired up bunch of guys. Needless to say we came out in the second half and won the game 37-7,[18] earning ourselves a rematch against LSU in the Sugar Bowl.[19] I've often wondered what would have happened had Robert not made that remarkable kick.

---

[17] This title is the equivalent of the most popular male student at Ole Miss.

[18] Ole Miss entered this game ranked fifth, but that decisive win catapulted the Rebels to the number two spot in the nation. How Ole Miss and LSU Advanced to the 1960 Sugar Bowl, Official Site of the Allstate Sugar Bowl, http://www.allstatesugarbowl.org/site216.php (last visited Aug. 1, 2011).

[19] The Ole Miss Rebels handily defeated the LSU Tigers 21-0 for their first National Championship. The 1960 Sugar Bowl was the first bowl game nationally

At the end of the football season, Robert was selected to play in the College All-Star Game against the NFL's reigning champion, the Baltimore Colts.[20] Robert remembers playing this game not as a kicker but as an offensive lineman. He loves to tell the story of lining up for the first play from scrimmage and across from him was none other than the Colts' All-Pro defensive tackle Eugene "Big Daddy" Lipscomb.[21] Lipscomb, who was listed at 6'7," 300-plus pounds, looked across the line at Robert and said, "Boy, does your mamma know where you are?" Robert replied, "Obviously not. If she did I would still be in Moss Point!" I guess you could call his reply *grace under pressure*. The fact that Robert chose to kick in the NFL is a testament to his intelligence.[22]

After an excellent career in professional football, Robert returned to Oxford and, as we all know, began his journey to becoming the fifteenth chancellor of the University of Mississippi. Those of us who love Ole Miss are grateful to him for being there for us and helping make our alma mater become the wonderful place that it is today. A few years ago, Robert's good friend and former law school student, John Grisham was giving a talk on campus and he said, "When I grow up, I want to be just like Robert Khayat."[23] For those of us who have known and loved Robert for so many years, I think that just about sums up our feelings. We should all want to grow up to be like Robert Khayat.

---

televised in color. 26th Annual Sugar Bowl Classic ~ January 1, 1960, Official Site of the Allstate Sugar Bowl, http://www.allstatesugarbowl.org/site140.php (last visited Aug. 1, 2011).

[20] This game was known as The Chicago Charities College All-Star Game, and was held from 1934 to 1976 at Soldier Field in Chicago. The 1960 All-Star game featured Johnny Unitas throwing three touchdown passes to lead the Colts to a 32-7 victory over the College All-Stars and their coach, Otto Graham. Mark Bolding, *The 1960 College All-star Game*, BOLDING SPORTS RESEARCH, http://www.mmbolding.com/BSR/The_Chicago_All-Star_Game_1960.htm (last visited Aug. 1, 2011).

[21] Eugene "Big Daddy" Lipscomb played ten seasons in the National Football League and was selected for the Pro Bowl three times. Lipscomb played defensive tackle for the Los Angeles Rams, the Baltimore Colts, and the Pittsburgh Steelers. William Nack, *The Ballad of Big Daddy*, SPORTS ILLUSTRATED, Jan. 11, 1999, at 72-88.

[22] Robert Khayat played four seasons for the Washington Redskins, and was named to the Pro Bowl in 1961. THE NATIONAL FOOTBALL FOUNDATION, http://www.footballfoundation.org/nff/biography/828/dr-robert-c-khayat (last visited Aug. 1, 2011).

[23] John R. Grisham, Address at the Investiture Ceremony of Chancellor Robert C. Khayat (Apr. 11, 1996).

### DEAN EMERITUS PARHAM H. WILLIAMS JR.*

The morning was sunny, warm, and pleasantly humid—a typical September morning in Oxford. I carefully opened my Criminal Law casebook on the podium and surveyed the thirty-one students gathered for the first class of the semester. All were males who sat quietly, apprehensive and uncertain of what to expect. My eyes settled on a young giant squeezed into a narrow seat in the second row. Beneath his blond buzz cut, two baby blues gazed at me expectantly. "Aha," I thought, "this must be Khayat." Everyone on the law faculty knew who Khayat was—All-American, All-Pro, Colonel Rebel, Hall of Fame, frequent escort of Miss Americas and other glamour queens—but we were uncertain of his talent for serious academic work. I decided to test the waters.

"Mr. Khayat," I said in a tone of soothing insouciance, "our first case is *Barker v. State*.[24] Would you be so kind as to recount the facts and then analyze the court's holding?"

The case was a time bomb, loaded with conflicting facts and confusing definitions of the degrees of murder. I smiled inwardly, expecting a floundering effort that would expose the student's total ineptitude for the study of law.

The response stunned me. The recounting of the facts was thorough and explicit. Some stumbling did occur in unraveling the theories of homicide, but few lawyers would have done any better. I regarded "Mister" Khayat with a growing sense of appreciation.

This guy was smart!

Thus unfolded my introduction to Robert Khayat, the law student. My initial impressions were continually reinforced as I

---

* Parham H. Williams Jr.: B.A., University of Mississippi; J.D., University of Mississippi; LL.M., Yale University. Dean Emeritus Parham Williams served as associate dean of the University of Mississippi School of Law in 1970 and dean of the school from 1971 to 1985. In 1985, Dean Williams left the university to serve as the dean of the Cumberland School of Law at Samford University in Birmingham, Alabama. After eleven years in that position, Dean Williams moved to Chapman University School of Law in Orange, California to lead that school as dean. Following his retirement from Chapman, Dean Williams returned to the University of Mississippi School of Law where he continues to teach. The Dean Parham H. Williams Endowed Scholarship has been established at each of the three schools of law led by Dean Williams and each school continues to award students with that scholarship.

[24] 150 N.E.2d 680 (1958).

got to know Robert better. He proved to be an excellent student, always well-prepared and ready to offer thoughtful comments and useful analyses of legal issues. Equally impressive was his willingness to undertake special assignments, whether curricular or extra-curricular (Josh Morse and Bill Bunkley had a few of the latter),[25] and to accomplish them quickly and effectively. I was not surprised when he was selected for membership on the *Mississippi Law Journal,* nor when I learned that his law school GPA ranked near the top of his class.

I doubt that many people today know that, while yet a student, Robert "created" the Ole Miss Law Alumni Chapter. I well remember when Josh Morse, then dean of the law school, asked Robert to "see if you can dig up the names of our graduates and make me a list." Not only did Robert "dig up the names," he created a complete directory including the address, age, and year of graduation of every living Ole Miss law graduate. Then he arranged the initial meeting, counseled the newly elected officers, and guided the nascent organization in its developing years. Frankly, all of us who graduated from the law school are the beneficiaries of Robert's ground-breaking work in establishing an organization that continues to provide invaluable support to the law school and the bar.

After I became dean, I was truly privileged to have Robert's unfailing assistance and support as associate dean. When I reflect on those years (it seems that I spend a lot of time reflecting these days!), I inevitably conclude that much of the success achieved by the law school during those years was the result of Robert's inspired and untiring efforts in coordinating the academic work of the faculty and students. He was the quintessential role model for our younger law faculty—an exceptionally able and conscientious classroom teacher; a productive scholar; and a compassionate and caring counselor and friend to his students. In addition to carrying a full teaching load, Robert was incredibly productive as an administrator, carrying more than his full share of administrative duties while accomplishing unbelievable quantities of just plain

---

[25] Both men were dean of the University of Mississippi School of Law. Joshua M. Morse served as dean from 1963 to 1969, while Joel W. Bunkley, Jr., served as dean from 1969 to 1971. MICHAEL DE L. LANDON, THE UNIVERSITY OF MISSISSIPPI SCHOOL OF LAW: A SESQUICENTENNIAL HISTORY 97, 112-113, 118 (2006).

old hard work. I shall always be grateful for Robert's support and help.

Few university presidents have graced their office with the array of skills and experience that Robert exemplified. True, some presidents may match his "people skills"—though close inspection will narrow that list to a handful. And granted, some may boast of comparable campus building programs—though again I suspect that the list is quite short. And there may be a few, a very few, with the incredible talent for fundraising that is among Robert's most notable strengths. But none, I am certain, have encouraged and influenced more people with the warm and winsome sincerity that is the hallmark of his very being.

Let's cut to the chase. How many university presidents have been at the helm of their school when it achieved a coveted chapter of Phi Beta Kappa? And how many have raised hundreds of millions in gifts that have transformed their institution? And how many have presided over a presidential debate?[26] And how many can stand shoulder-to-shoulder with Marty Stuart and blow away the crowd with scintillating Nashville chops and rockabilly chicken pickin'?[27] I rest my case.

Prime among Robert's virtues are an easy grace and an innate modesty. But he deserves to enjoy the accolades heaped upon him, especially the naming of this magnificent law center in his honor. Consider this. When Dean Roscoe Pound finally retired as university professor at Harvard in 1947, a collection of essays, penned by the leading scholars of the day, was published in his honor. A magazine reporter asked him his thoughts about the publication. The venerable dean smiled and replied: "Well, a man is entitled to have his head swell a little over that!"[28] So, my counsel to Robert is simple: let your head "swell just a little bit"

---

[26] On September 26, 2008, the University of Mississippi hosted the first in a series of four presidential debates between Senator John McCain and then Senator Barack Obama. 2008 PRESIDENTIAL DEBATE, http://www.olemiss.edu/debate/ (last visited Aug. 1, 2011).

[27] Country music singer Marty Stuart wrote *The Moss Point Kid* as a tribute to then Chancellor Khayat. Stuart performed the song during a concert at the Gertrude Ford Center on April 30, 2009. MARTY STUART, *The Moss Point Kid* (2009). A video of the performance is available at: http://www.youtube.com/watch?v=E0v2qDHAgyo (last visited Aug. 1, 2011).

[28] *Education: Man with a Memory*, TIME MAGAZINE (Feb. 24, 1947), at 50.

and enjoy all the good words that come your way. And please know always that I am very, very proud to have been your teacher, your colleague, and your friend.

## THE HONORABLE REUBEN V. ANDERSON[*]

Robert Khayat and I were students in law school together at the University of Mississippi in the mid-1960s. I can say with all honesty that not everyone greeted me with the same ready smile and handshake that he did. Many did not acknowledge my existence. That was the beginning of my deep respect for this man.

Over the more than forty-five years that I have known Robert Khayat, I have had many opportunities to witness his immensely significant contributions to the university, the legal profession, and the State of Mississippi. I have known him in his capacity as a professor at the law school and as university chancellor. Throughout my legal career, our paths have crossed many times. This tribute gives me the chance to offer a public thanks for the many considerate acts of kindness he has provided me.

I would like to reflect, however, on more personal experiences that reveal his generosity of spirit and fullness of character. What I have seen him do for our state as a whole is remarkable. We have worked together with the Mississippi Economic Council, our state's premier economic development organization. He took on the challenging task of leading the first Blueprint Mississippi

---

[*] Reuben Anderson is a senior litigation partner in the Jackson office of Phelps Dunbar LLP. Prior to joining Phelps Dunbar, Mr. Anderson served as the first African-American Justice on the Mississippi Supreme Court. Mr. Anderson grew up in Jackson and graduated from Tougaloo College in 1964. After being denied admission into the University of Mississippi School of Law, Anderson enrolled in law school at Southern University in Baton Rouge. After his first year, Anderson received a scholarship to the University of Mississippi School of Law where he was the only African-American student in his class.

Upon graduation, Mr. Anderson was hired by the NAACP Legal Defense Fund where he focused his practice on school desegregation and civil rights. In 1970, Mr. Anderson helped form the law firm of Anderson Banks Nichols & Leventhal. Jackson mayor, Russell Davis, appointed Anderson municipal court judge in 1976. Governor Clifton "Cliff" Finch appointed Anderson County Court Judge in 1977. In 1981, Governor William Winter appointed Anderson to the Hinds County Circuit Court, and in 1985, he was appointed by Governor William Allain to the Mississippi Supreme Court. Anderson served in that capacity for six years.

Throughout his professional career, Mr. Anderson served as president of the Mississippi Economic Council, president of the Mississippi Bar Association, and a commissioner for the National Collegiate Athletic Association. He was inducted into the Ole Miss Alumni Hall of Fame in 1995 and received the Distinguished Alumnus Award. Mr. Anderson received a Mississippi Bar Lifetime Achievement Award in 2007 as well as the University of Mississippi School of Law Alumnus of the Year Award in 2005.

effort,[29] pulling together a somewhat fragmented business community and creating a common agenda.

The final report released in 2004 was a strategic business plan for continuous and significant improvements in the standard of living across all regions of Mississippi.[30] It called for ways to nurture the business climate, improve education, and advance economic development through a partnership between business, education, and government, so that all of the goals outlined in the plan could be achieved. As a result of the thorough planning the initiatives have been sustained. This is a product of the time and effort that Robert Khayat put into the task.

Another noteworthy accomplishment that I witnessed is the part he played in reaching a resolution of the *Ayers* case regarding state funding for historically black universities, long neglected.[31] It was at his suggestion, as chancellor of Ole Miss, that the Board of Trustees of State Institutions of Higher Learning reached an agreement that helped bring an end to the litigation and direct funds to Jackson State University, Alcorn State University, and Mississippi Valley State University. Without his influence, the matter could be still in litigation.

His close association with the University of Mississippi Medical Center in its academic as well as health care roles, including its presence at the Jackson Medical Mall, has been a tremendous benefit to the city of Jackson and the State of Mississippi. The new Ole Miss Chancellor, Dr. Daniel Jones, is maintaining the same strong support, and the university's supporters appreciate this thoughtful plan of succession.

---

[29] Blueprint Mississippi is a coalition of state development agencies whose mission is to "[t]o create a strategic business plan, a blueprint, that provides opportunity for continuous and significant improvements in the standard of living across all regions of Mississippi. This sustainable, trackable program of work will serve as a road map to success by nurturing the business climate, improving education and advancing economic development through a partnership among business, education and government."

[30] A link to the full text as well as an executive summary of the 2004 report can be found at: http://www.msmec.com/images/stories/blueprint/2004BlueprintReport.pdf

[31] The *Ayers* case refers to a settlement reached between the State, the Justice Department, and private plaintiffs in a suit filed by Jake Ayers, Sr., claiming that the state's historically black colleges suffered from not receiving the same funding as the State's historically white colleges. The settlement resulted in the State agreeing to spend nearly $500 million over two decades to increase funding for Jackson State University, Alcorn State University, and Mississippi Valley State University.

All of us in this state—businesses, educational institutions, and citizens—have also benefitted from Robert Khayat's influence in Washington, D.C., and the Mississippi State Capitol. And we will all benefit for generations to come, as graduates of the University of Mississippi and its school of law gain valuable skills and knowledge for their lives and careers, thanks to the superb advancements both institutions have enjoyed under Robert Khayat's leadership. His integrity, vision, and perseverance are the hallmarks of leadership of the highest order.

PROFESSOR ROBERT A. WEEMS*

I would never have taught at the University of Mississippi School of Law but for Robert Khayat. I met Robert when I came to law school in 1964. He had started the previous semester. We became good friends, as did our wives. Following our graduation we kept in close touch. After practicing law in Pascagoula for a while, he joined the faculty of the law school, and soon became associate dean. He would mention from time to time that he thought I would like teaching law, and that there was a possibility of joining the faculty at Ole Miss. I had been in private practice in Vicksburg for eleven years, but the thought of teaching at Ole Miss certainly peaked my interest. When I told Robert that I would like to try, he, with the assistance of other friends on the faculty like Guff Abbott, Cliff Hodge,[32] and Dean Parham Williams, got the rest of the faculty to go along.

My tenure at the law school, however, may well have been short-lived but for Robert. I had been teaching Wills and Estates, and had developed cases, statutes, and materials for a new course specific to Mississippi wills and estates. Under the prevailing rules at the time, this compilation alone was sufficient to satisfy the research component required for tenure, however, the year that I became eligible for tenure the university hired a new provost who instituted new tenure requirements. His rule was that a candidate for tenure had to publish a book or some other significant work—which left me understandably concerned. The day after hearing of this new rule, Robert informed me that we were flying to Atlanta the next day to talk to the people at The Harrison Company, publishers of law books. He, with the

---

* Robert A. Weems: B.S., Millsaps College; J.D., University of Mississippi. Professor Weems joined the faculty of the University of Mississippi School of Law in 1977. Since then he has been named Outstanding Law Professor six times and received the university's Outstanding Teacher Award in 1994. Professor Weems has published multiple editions of the books Wills and Administration of Estates in Mississippi and Mississippi Wills and Estates: Cases, Statutes, and Materials. Along with Professor Emeritus Guthrie T. Abbott, Professor Weems conducted the annual seminar "Summary of Recent Mississippi Law" from 1984 to 2011.

[32] E. Clifton Hodge, Jr., served as an associate professor with the University of Mississippi School of Law from 1974 to 1982. Mr. Hodge is currently a partner in the general litigation group of the law firm Phelps Dunbar LLP in Jackson, Mississippi. PHELPS DUNBAR, http://www.phelpsdunbar.com/attorney-profile/profile/hodgejr-94.html (last visited Aug. 1, 2011).

assistance of Dean Williams, got them to agree to publish my book so that I could qualify for tenure—which I got.[33] Robert was not only considerate of his friends, but was always willing to use his influence and charm to help anyone who could use it.

Robert contributed to the betterment of the law school in countless ways. He was a very good teacher. His special expertise was in local government law. His students loved him for his teaching ability and perhaps even more for his interest in them as individuals as well as students. By the middle of a semester he would know them all by name and know something about most of them. And it seems he never forgot.

He also made many meaningful contributions to Oxford and Lafayette County. I will mention just two. Shortly after I had moved to Oxford I went with him on a Thursday night to Harmontown,[34] a small community north of Oxford, to explain to a group why he thought it was important for them to vote for a bond issue to renovate the courthouse on the Square in Oxford. Through Robert's help the initiative passed. He was also a moving force in getting a two percent tourism tax passed, over determined opposition, to help the university build a baseball stadium and to provide the City with funds to make it more attractive to visitors. To date, the City has received millions of dollars from this tax, and the baseball stadium we have now has grown from that beginning.[35]

But Robert's crowning achievements came during his fourteen-year tenure as chancellor of the university. It has been said that he did not just improve the university, but transformed it. He transformed the attitudes of many people who work here, and of the students who study here. He transformed the physical campus as well. There is no part of the university that was not improved, whether it was the construction of new buildings, the

---

[33] Professor Weems' book—MISSISSIPPI WILLS AND ESTATES: CASES, STATUTES, AND MATERIALS—was a huge success and in print for twenty years, producing three editions.

[34] Harmontown, Mississippi is an unincorporated community located in Lafayette County between Highway 7 and Interstate 55, just north of Sardis Lake.

[35] The current baseball facility, Swayze Field at Oxford-University Stadium, opened on February 19, 1989. OLEMISSSPORTS.COM, http://www.olemisssports.com/facilities/ole-facilities-swayze-field.html (last visited Aug. 1, 2011).

renovation of existing buildings, or the beautification of virtually every piece of ground not occupied by a building.

In Saint Paul's Cathedral in London there is a plaque bearing the name of its great architect, Sir Christopher Wren. It is inscribed "Reader, if you seek his memorial—look around you."[36] There easily could be a plaque like that somewhere, anywhere, on this campus with Robert Khayat's name on it.

---

[36] The Latin phrase etched on a stone plaque obituary by Wren's son, reads "Lector, Si Monumentum Requiris Circumspice." JAMES ELMES, SIR CHRISTOPHER WREN AND HIS TIMES 411 (Chapman & Hall 1852).

## Professor Emeritus Guthrie T. Abbott[*]

In 1964, my wife and I, newlyweds, moved into the Avent Acres apartments in Oxford, Mississippi, and my life was changed for the better because that is where I met Robert Conrad Khayat. Robert and I were starting at the Ole Miss Law School. I entered law school because I couldn't figure out what to do with my math degree, and Bob Galloway,[37] my good friend and college roommate, was going to law school—so why not just tag along?

Robert entered law school because he needed help with the laws of contracts–especially negotiations. You see, Robert had just finished a year of work as placekicker for the Washington Redskins of the NFL. For his excellent work, Robert was awarded All-Pro honors by the league, and the Redskins offered him a contract for about $14,000 to sign for the next year. Robert, without the help of the sports agent who is so ubiquitous today, demanded that he be paid $15,000, or "I will just go to law school." The rest is history! The Redskins had another bad year, and the University of Mississippi and our law school continue to reap the benefits of the Redskins' folly.

Knowing Robert as a neighbor, law school classmate, faculty colleague, and as chancellor, has enriched my life in many ways. He has always been an exemplar of what a fine human being should be. Of course, his shining examples kept many of us Avent Acres neighbors in trouble by comparison. For instance, on cold winter mornings when my wife Patsy would go out to start our car

---

[*] Guthrie T. (Guff) Abbott: B.A., University of Mississippi; J.D., University of Mississippi; Fellow in Law and the Humanities, Harvard University. Professor Abbott became a full-time member of the University of Mississippi School of Law faculty in 1970 following three years of private practice in Gulfport, Mississippi. From 1984 to 2011 Professor Abbott, in conjunction with Professor Robert Weems, conducted the annual seminar "Summary of Recent Mississippi Law." Professor Abbott served as the acting dean of the law school from 1985 to 1986, and in 1998 became the second professor to serve as the president of the Mississippi Bar following Dean Robert J. Farley who served as bar president in 1954. Professor Abbott is the Butler, Snow, O'Mara, Stevens, & Cannada Lecturer in Law Emeritus and continues to teach Mississippi Civil Practice at the school of law.

[37] Robert C. Galloway is a member of Butler, Snow, O'Mara, Stevens, & Cannada, PLLC in the firm's Gulfport office. Mr. Galloway received his bachelor's degree from the University of Mississippi in 1964, followed by a law degree from the University of Mississippi School of Law in 1967. BUTLER SNOW, http://www.butlersnow.com/bob_galloway.aspx (last visited Aug. 1, 2011).

and go to work, she would see that Robert's long green Pontiac was running and getting warm for Margaret Khayat to enter shortly thereafter. My mother taught me that "comparisons were odious," but Patsy was obviously never given that lesson.

Robert was a leader at the law school from the day that he joined the faculty, and I will forever be indebted to him for helping me gain a faculty position. There are numerous reasons why Robert was well-liked and respected by students and faculty alike, but a conversation that we had many years ago explains a lot. Robert was serving as associate dean of the law school and had just helped a student stay in school by both securing financial aid and sharing some sound advice regarding school and life.[38] As with so many other instances in assisting students and faculty colleagues, Robert had gone "above and beyond." I tried to compliment Robert on what he had done, but he wouldn't hear of it. He simply said: "Guff, what I really like to do is help people."

Well Robert has been blessed and in turn has blessed thousands of people with his help, including me. His innovative thinking, sound judgment, and work ethic have benefitted the law school, the university, the legal profession, and our community and state.

I am literally "richer" because of Robert. In my thirties Robert *made me* start saving some money. He said: "Guff, you owe it to your family. You have to save something every month, even if it is just $50.00." I listened, and we may never be rich, but we will never be poor—thanks to Robert Khayat.

In discussing Robert with faculty colleagues you hear of his wonderful sense of humor (he even laughed when referred to as the "Ass Dean" of the law school—short for Associate Dean, of course). Words and phrases such as: "collegial," "forgiving" (I do not believe that Robert has ever held a grudge in his life), "caring," "sound judgment," "fair," "smart," "forward thinker," "truly loves and cares for all of God's children," are the types of comments you will hear.

---

[38] Robert Khayat served as the associate dean of the law school for seven years before moving to the Lyceum to become vice chancellor for university affairs. Professor Thomas R. Mason would replace Khayat as the law school's associate dean. MICHAEL DE L. LANDON, THE UNIVERSITY OF MISSISSIPPI SCHOOL OF LAW: A SESQUICENTENNIAL HISTORY 144 (2006).

It is my privilege to know and be influenced by Robert and to call him colleague and friend. I smile every time I enter the Robert C. Khayat Law Center. No honor ever bestowed could be more richly deserved.

## JUDGE S. ALLAN ALEXANDER*

I never knew Robert Khayat the football player, perish the thought! Football? I attended a small undergraduate school for women in Missouri, if that gives any indication of my interest in sports. I met "Mr. Khayat" as a first-year student at the law school in 1975, but I was never in one of his classes. After graduating from law school and working for two years as a federal law clerk, I went into private practice as an associate with Holcomb, Dunbar, Connell, Merkel, Tollison, & Khayat, where Robert was a partner. By that time, however, Robert was spending almost all of his time as a law professor, so I never actually practiced law with him.

All of those "near misses" would ordinarily mean that Robert Khayat had no opportunity or inclination to influence me personally or professionally, but that is not the case. In fact, his grace and example have been guideposts for me, more and more as I have grown older.

The size of the law school student body population has not changed much since the mid-seventies. I was in the last class to graduate from Farley Hall;[39] the cramped building somehow felt more intimate and allowed more constant interaction between faculty and students. It will not surprise anyone who ever met Robert to learn that he took advantage of that fact, always making a point to learn students' names and something about them personally. He has always had that rare gift that allows him to connect with and motivate other people regardless of gender, race, age or socioeconomic status. He regularly mingled with students in the halls, visited the *Law Journal* offices (and, I'm sure, other student-staffed offices) to take our pulses and generally let all the

---

* Judge S. Allan Alexander: B.A., William Woods College; J.D., University of Mississippi. Following fourteen years of private practice in Oxford, Mississippi, Judge Alexander was appointed to her current position as a United States Magistrate Judge for the Northern District of Mississippi in 1994. Since 2007, Judge Alexander has served as a co-chairperson of the uniform local civil rules committee for the United States District Courts for the Northern and Southern Districts of Mississippi, and since 2008, she has served as the chairperson of the rules committee for the Federal Magistrate Judges Association. In 2008 Judge Alexander was bestowed with the Mississippi Women Lawyers Association Lifetime Achievement Award and in 2009 received the Northern District Chief Judge Award.

[39] The University of Mississippi School of Law moved from Farley Hall to the Lamar Law Center in the summer of 1978. *See* MICHAEL DE L. LANDON, THE UNIVERSITY OF MISSISSIPPI SCHOOL OF LAW: A SESQUICENTENNIAL HISTORY 136 (2006).

students know that he was available to assist them in any way he could.[40] He still calls me "Miss A." because my first-year study group—a group of what my mother always referred to as "knotheads"—called me that. Everyone in the study group but me played guitar or banjo, and Robert used to bring his guitar when they got together to celebrate and play. We loved that.

Although Robert's life may appear charmed to some, his successes have come to him not by luck but by dint of good instincts, a head for strategy, a sense of mission, and the hard work and dedication necessary to carry him to full success in nearly everything he has ever attempted. His keen powers of observation and his insight into human nature, in combination with his determination to excel while doing good, give him the vision to see possibilities and the energy to push them through to reality possessed by very few. It is our good fortune that he chose to apply all of these talents to the task of directing the University of Mississippi toward excellence in all departments. It is no exaggeration to say that there was probably no other individual who in fourteen short years could have moved Ole Miss so far away from its haunted, negative past and started the school so effectively on its clear path to real academic competitiveness in a public university setting.

In all of his accomplishments Robert has been guided by a rock-solid sense of what is right and what is wrong. And he has learned—and taught me along the way—that inner peace and a constructive life come from forgiveness of self and, more importantly, forgiveness of others for real or perceived wrongs. As he once told me, refusal to forgive does nothing to harm the unforgiven; the harm it causes is to the intransigent grudge-holder, eating away at the latter's capacity for kindness and good. Life, he said, became so much simpler after he came to that realization. The concept that hatred and vengeance do not solve problems did not originate with Robert, of course, but he was the one who personified it for me by living the principle himself.

This, then, is the Robert Khayat I know. He is a mission-driven perfectionist with his drive tempered by a strong sense of

---

[40] While in law school, Judge Alexander served as Editor-in-Chief of the *Mississippi Law Journal*. 48 MISS. L.J. 1097 (1977).

compassion, fairness, and justice. His example has been invaluable to me and to countless others.

## Professor Deborah H. Bell[*]

I have known Robert Khayat as a colleague, a dean, and a chancellor. But I first knew him as my professor.

I started law school in 1976. It was a different time. Professor Kingsfield, of *The Paper Chase* fame,[41] was a model for law professors across the country. The Socratic method—overlaid with intimidation and, in some cases, sarcasm—was the expected style of teaching. Then, there were no laptops in the classroom. No barrier between you and the query with your name attached. No way for a compassionate classmate to text you a few key phrases. And the demographic of the faculty matched. The professors were male. White. Intimidating.[42]

The class of 1979 gathered for the first time in an enormous lecture hall—all 220 of us in a single Torts class. Looking back, I can see the faces of judges, governors, CEOs, bar presidents. But at 8:00 on an August morning, we were frightened twenty-somethings in faded jeans and bad 70s hair.[43] Tom Mason lit a cigarette,[44] waved a coffee cup at us, and in his gravely smoker's

---

[*] Professor Deborah Hodges Bell: J.D., University of Mississippi. A 1979 graduate of the University of Mississippi School of Law, Professor Bell joined the school's faculty in 1981. She is the founder of the school's Civil Legal Clinic and served as the clinic's director until 2009. Professor Bell is the author of the book *Bell on Mississippi Family Law*, currently in its second edition and widely used by the State's practitioners and judiciary. She has served on various statewide committees including the Access to Justice Commission Pro Se Committee, the Mississippi Gender Fairness Task Force, and the Supreme Court Domestic Violence Task Force. Professor Bell has received numerous awards including 2005 University of Mississippi Law Faculty Public Service Award, the 2006 Mississippi Bar Outstanding Woman Lawyer of the Year Award, 2007 Mississippi Center for Justice Champion of Justice Award, and the 2009 Mississippi Bar Susie Blue Buchanan Lifetime Award. As a student at the University of Mississippi School of Law, Bell served as the Editor-in-Chief of the *Mississippi Law Journal*.

[41] The 1973 film, based on the 1970 novel, starred John Houseman as Charles W. Kingsfield, Jr., the "boorish and pompous . . . [s]ocratic [m]onster" who served as the first-year Contracts professor at Harvard Law School. Michael Vitiello, *Professor Kingsfield: The Most misunderstood Character in Literature*, 33 HOFSTRA L. REV. 955, 966 (2005).

[42] Now we have gender equality—the Kingsfield role was effectively reprised by a woman in the movie *Legally Blonde* when she asked one student if he would bet a classmate's life on his answer. LEGALLY BLONDE (Metro-Goldwyn-Mayer 2001).

[43] The Farrah Fawcett "wings" look was the style of choice. Somehow it never looked like the poster.

[44] Thomas R. Mason joined the faculty of the University of Mississippi School of Law in the spring of 1973 and was appointed associate dean in the fall of 1983.

voice said, "Girl in the black t-shirt . . . stand up."[45] My heart stopped. My voice shook.[46] Property was no better. I spent hours preparing my case presentation for "Iron" Mike Featherstone—complete with a diagram for the board.[47] He picked up an eraser, wiped away my notes and told me to sit down. I knew classmates who were physically ill before his class.

Having survived round one, we gathered for the first spring class in the strange first-floor room with the enormous column in the middle.[48] The schedule read Wills and Estates, Professor Robert Khayat. We all were, understandably, tense—girded for the next onslaught.

Robert's teaching style was by far the friendliest and most relaxed we had encountered. The class was challenging, but there was no shouting. He was firm without being demeaning. He expected much from us . . . but he offered something in return. He remembered our names. He wanted to know about our hometowns. He asked about—and often knew—our parents. And, over the years, he never forgot us.

Robert has described the significance of one person's friendliness to him as a lonely, homesick freshman. He has done the same for more students than we can count. Fittingly, the building that bears his name is designed for connection. The classrooms encourage exchange rather than create intimidation. The building is scattered with small group seating. Student organization offices are scattered among faculty offices, and a café

---

MICHAEL DE L. LANDON, THE UNIVERSITY OF MISSISSIPPI SCHOOL OF LAW: A SESQUICENTENNIAL HISTORY 123, 144 (2006).

[45] Professors were free to smoke in class, including George Cochran, who repeatedly confused his cigarette with chalk and stabbed the blackboard, shooting sparks into the first row of the class.

[46] Professor Mason's growl, it turned out, disguised an Okie heart of gold. But it took a while to realize that.

[47] D. Michael Featherstone joined the faculty of the law school in 1972 and would remain with the school for twenty-nine years before retiring in 2001. David W. Case, *Tribute to "Iron Mike" Featherstone*, 70 MISS. L.J. 497 (2000).

[48] Tommy Ethridge, whom we miss dearly, is alleged to have called repeatedly during one semester on "Mr. Post," misreading the designation for the column on the seating chart.

Thomas R. Ethridge joined the law school faculty in 1971 following his service as a Mississippi State Senator and a United States attorney for the northern district of Mississippi. MICHAEL DE L. LANDON, THE UNIVERSITY OF MISSISSIPPI SCHOOL OF LAW: A SESQUICENTENNIAL HISTORY 117 (2006).

offers a spot for faculty and students to mingle throughout the day. Even the staircases seem designed to make us stop and talk.

Robert's achievements as chancellor have been aptly documented. He will be remembered for the beauty of the campus, the expansion of private funding, securing Phi Beta Kappa, recruiting minority students. But what I will remember is that as a first-year law student he made me feel at home.[49]

---

[49] And oddly, it has turned out to be just that.

MARY ANN CONNELL*

Chancellor Robert C. Khayat and I first met in the Sunday school class for freshmen students in Wesley Hall at the Oxford-University Methodist Church in early September 1956. I was a sophomore at the university attending the Sunday school class for a second year because Dean Malcolm Guess, the teacher, told my friend Mary Ann Mobley and me that we had failed the class the first time around and had to pay penance by coming back the second year to welcome and assist the next class of incoming freshmen. On the first Sunday of the fall semester in 1956, we welcomed the new group to our class with donuts and hot chocolate. Among the group were Dan Jordan from Philadelphia and two young men from South Mississippi, Robert Khayat and Warner Alford. Also in the class were Gerald Walton, later provost of the university, and his to-be wife, Julie Hart. That nurturing and supportive place spawned friendships that would last a lifetime.

Throughout our days at Ole Miss, I observed Chancellor Khayat to be the same warm, loving, caring, and charismatic person he is today. A true "Renaissance Man," he studied history and literature, read and wrote poetry, appreciated music and the arts, and engaged in the life of the university community in all of its multi-faceted layers. He was the embodiment of what the study of liberal arts is about.

My first professional interaction with Chancellor Khayat came when he, Grady Tollison, and I practiced law together on the Square in Oxford. Although it was a time when women were not generally accepted in the legal world, they welcomed me, taught me how to practice law, supported me intellectually and personally, and caused me to love being a part of the legal profession.

Our lives continued to intersect professionally and personally. Shortly after Chancellor Khayat returned to the

---

* Mary Ann Connell: B.A., University of Mississippi; M.A., University of Mississippi; MLSci., University of Mississippi; J.D., University of Mississippi; LL.M., Harvard Law School. Ms. Connell was formerly general counsel for the University of Mississippi and a former president of the National Association of College and University Attorneys. She is presently of counsel with Mayo Mallette PLLC, Oxford, Mississippi.

campus to teach in the law school, I became the university attorney. I continued to see the boy-student of early Ole Miss days grow to become the man-student of later professor and chancellor days. Through all these years, I have continued to observe the eternal verities of William Faulkner—truth, justice, mercy, kindness, and love—lived out in this person whom I am honored to call my friend.

In 1969, Chancellor Khayat and his wife Margaret moved to Oxford shortly after my husband Bill and I did. Chancellor Khayat and I immediately restored our college friendship, but this time with an added dimension. I found Chancellor Khayat's wife Margaret to be my soul-mate. From the beginning of our friendship, we recognized that we are different in many ways, but those differences do not matter. We share a binding, loving relationship that ideological and political differences can never separate. She is one of the brightest, quickest, most well-read, interesting, loving, caring people I have ever known. Time spent with Margaret is time cherished by me. So, to Chancellor Khayat, I give my appreciation for bringing a true friend, Margaret, into my life.

Although Chancellor Khayat's accomplishments as chancellor are many, one in particular has provided the university with tremendous national recognition and will endure in perpetuity.

In his investiture address on April 11, 1996, Chancellor Khayat "set for the institution a series of goals that would improve the academic quality of the University of Mississippi, [and] stimulate the intellectual and cultural life of the university community. . . ."[50] One of his most ambitious goals was to pursue a long-held dream of *sheltering* a chapter of Phi Beta Kappa.[51] Many, including the chancellor's strongest supporters, thought he was dreaming the impossible.[52]

---

[50] *Robert C. Khayat Investiture Address*, OXFORD EAGLE, Apr. 11, 1996, at 11B.

[51] *Id.* The term "shelter" is used by Phi Beta Kappa to indicate that a college or university hosts a chapter of the academic fraternity.

[52] *See, e.g.*, Barbara Lago, *The Renaissance Man*, 54 OLE MISS ALUMNI REV. 24 (Summer 2005) (Gloria Kellum, vice chancellor for university relations, stated "When he unfolded his plans to pursue a chapter, I told him he was crazy, it was not possible. . . ."); Pamela Hamilton, *Accomplishment silences doubters*, DAILY MISSISSIPPIAN, Oct. 23, 2000, at 5 (noting that Chancellor Khayat admitted that "some people thought I'd lost my mind").

Chancellor Khayat displayed unwavering commitment and courage in an effort to obtain recognition by the nation's most prestigious academic honor society. Shortly after his appointment as the University of Mississippi's 15th chancellor, Chancellor Khayat called upon Dr. Douglas W. Foard, Secretary of the Phi Beta Kappa Society, in Washington, D.C., to discuss how the university might succeed in its application for a chapter of Phi Beta Kappa and why the university's previous applications had been denied.[53]

Dr. Foard told Chancellor Khayat that the university's library holdings were inadequate, faculty salaries in the College of Liberal Arts were below standard, and student ACT scores were too low.[54] Dr. Foard also impressed upon the chancellor that the application for a chapter must originate with and be submitted by the faculty of the university who were members of Phi Beta Kappa. When he returned to Oxford, Chancellor Khayat first set about to remedy the problems Dr. Foard had identified. He solicited gifts from generous donors: $8 million to support the holdings of the John D. Williams Library, $5.4 million to recreate the honors program as the Sally McDonnell Barksdale Honors College,[55] a gift equivalent to a $60 million endowment to create the Croft Institute for International Studies, $30 million from two former law students as an endowment for faculty salaries, and a $25 million commitment from the Gertrude C. Ford Foundation for a state-of-the-art performing arts center.[56]

The University of Mississippi Foundation Board of Directors enthusiastically undertook responsibility for planning and

---

[53] Phi Beta Kappa rejected the university's previous applications in 1952, 1977, 1983, and 1987. The university withdrew its pending application with the outbreak of the Civil War. Likewise, the university withdrew its application in 1930 when Governor Bilbo intruded into higher education in Mississippi and dismissed several faculty members. Phi Beta Kappa suspended action on all applications, including that of the University of Mississippi, in 1942 after the beginning of World War II.

[54] Interview with Robert C. Khayat (Mar. 30, 2011); 54 OLE MISS ALUMNI REV. 27 (Summer 2005).

[55] A later endowment by the Barksdales brought the total gift to $8.3 million for continued support of the Honors College. The Honors College has housed some of the most gifted undergraduate students in the nation, including two Truman Scholars, two Goldwater Scholars, and a Rhodes Scholar.

[56] Interview with Robert C. Khayat (May 7, 2011); Interview with Don L. Fruge, former president and CEO of the University of Mississippi Foundation (May 2, 2011).

conducting a campaign for the private support that would fund academic enrichment projects for the library, scholarships, faculty salaries, and the honors program. The Phil Hardin Foundation provided a grant of $24,000 to support the work of the Phi Beta Kappa Application Committee and subsequently gave a $450,000 challenge grant to the university to be used in pursuit of a Phi Beta Kappa chapter.[57]

After obtaining these gift commitments, Chancellor Khayat hosted a dinner at Memory House for the thirty-five regular and six emeriti Phi Beta Kappa faculty members at the university and asked if they were willing to undertake leadership in the arduous process of applying for a chapter. The assembled faculty accepted Chancellor Khayat's challenge, and thus began an unprecedented partnership, including Chancellor Khayat, the university administration, the foundation, the faculty, staff, alumni, and friends of Ole Miss. With the endorsement of the Phi Beta Kappa faculty, Chancellor Khayat asked Dr. Ronald Schroeder, associate professor of English, to serve as chair of the Phi Beta Kappa Faculty Application Committee. Dr. Schroeder readily accepted and began work on the preliminary application. Chancellor Khayat offered the logistical support of the Office of the University Attorney toward compiling the massive amounts of data required. Nearly a year was spent gathering information and writing the preliminary application.

Chancellor Khayat and Dr. Schroeder delivered the university's 108-page preliminary application to the Phi Beta Kappa Society's Washington, D.C. headquarters on October 22, 1997.[58] When they returned to campus, Dr. Schroeder wrote Chancellor Khayat expressing his gratitude for the chancellor's "unflagging support of our application for a chapter of Phi Beta

---

[57] Letter from C. Thompson Waycaster to Chancellor Robert Khayat, Feb. 13, 1996 (on file in the office of the chancellor); *UM receives challenge grant to help obtain Phi Beta Kappa chapter*, OXFORD EAGLE, Oct. 10, 1997 (The challenge grant required the university to match the grant on a two-to-one basis. The university raised $900,000 to be eligible to receive the $450,000 grant.).

[58] Letter from Dr. Ronald A. Schroeder to The Committee on Qualifications, Phi Beta Kappa (Oct. 22, 1997) (on file in the office of the chancellor); memorandum from Dr. Ronald A. Schroeder to Phi Beta Kappa Faculty (Oct. 23, 1997) (on file in the office of the chancellor).

Kappa."[59] In particular, he thanked the chancellor for having given the Application Committee material assistance (notably by enlisting the university attorney to give logistical support), focusing the community's attention on the academic mission of the university, vigorously pursuing gifts and grants from external sources, and tirelessly offering encouragement and optimism.[60]

The preliminary application was well-received. Work immediately began on a much longer and comprehensive General Report that contained detailed information regarding virtually every facet of the university's mission and operation.[61]

The collaborative work in compiling this document took an entire year. On September 30, 1998, Dr. Schroeder delivered the 418-page General Report to the Phi Beta Kappa Society. The Society's Committee on Qualifications gave its preliminary approval of the written application. Shortly thereafter, a team of visitors from Phi Beta Kappa came to campus.[62] Over three days, they conducted an extensive study of the university's resources that supported the application for a chapter. Impressed with the

---

[59] Letter from Dr. Ronald A. Schroeder to Dr. Robert C. Khayat, chancellor (Oct. 23, 1997) (on file in the office of the university attorney).

[60] *Id.* It should be noted that during this same time period, Chancellor Khayat faced the greatest challenge of his years as chancellor. He upheld the ban the athletic department placed on sticks and banners exceeding 11" x 14" from athletic arenas as part of its game-management practice. This action was part of the chancellor's mission to change the image of the University of Mississippi by aggressively confronting its shortcomings, both real and perceived. His efforts resulted in Confederate flags almost totally disappearing from Vaught-Hemingway Stadium on football game days. *See* Kevin Sack, *The Final Refrains of "Dixie,"* N.Y. TIMES, Nov. 1, 1998, § 4A, at 20. The importance of Chancellor Khayat's action in the flag controversy cannot be overemphasized. *See* Lago, *supra* note 5, at 29 ("'Had we not dealt with the Rebel flag, we would not have received Phi Beta Kappa, and that is a fact,' Khayat said. 'I was told that by people in Phi Beta Kappa. That trauma we went through in '97 was part of this package.'"); *see also A legacy inscribed,* TUPELO DAILY J., Apr. 18, 2011, *available at* http://nems360.com/view/full_story/12830730/article-EDITORIAL—A-legacy-inscribed? ("The Phi Beta Kappa designation the university eventually received would not have come without those changes, nor would the university's heightened national profile.").

[61] The completed Report contained data on the organization of the university and the College of Liberal Arts, admission and enrollment of students, degrees conferred, the curriculum, grading policies, advising, cultural activities, faculty compensation, athletics, laboratories in the sciences, computing facilities, and the university's financial condition.

[62] Members of the visiting team were: Dr. Ira Fischler, psychology professor at the University of Florida; Dr. Allison Blakely, history professor at Howard University; and Dr. Solomon Gartenhaus, physics professor at Purdue University.

McDonnell-Barksdale Honors College; improved support for the libraries; the strengthening of the Liberal Arts faculty salaries; the diversity of the faculty, staff, and student body; and a rise in entering freshman ACT scores; the site team made a positive recommendation to Phi Beta Kappa's twelve-member Committee on Qualifications. In May 1999, the Committee on Qualifications recommended to the Phi Beta Kappa Senate that the faculty at the University of Mississippi shelter a chapter. The Senate followed the affirmative recommendation of the Committee and sent its positive vote to the Society's Council.

The final step in the process came on October 21, 2000, when Phi Beta Kappa Council delegates from all the chapters in the nation voted "overwhelmingly in favor" of establishing a chapter at the University of Mississippi.[63] Chancellor Khayat, Dr. Schroeder, and other representatives of the university were present at the national convention in Philadelphia, Pennsylvania, when the 300 delegates from around the country made the final vote. Within minutes after the affirmative vote was announced, Chancellor Khayat said: "I'm thrilled for the university and our students. It is really a national affirmation that Mississippi has made a major commitment to high-quality higher education."[64] One observer, describing the chancellor's jubilant spirit, said he looked "like the man who just kicked the winning field goal."[65]

Accolades and congratulations quickly poured in from faculty, students, alumni, donors, and officials at other universities. Phi Beta Kappa Society Secretary, Dr. Doug Foard praised the chancellor, saying: "Give Khayat the credit. He has brought the university to Phi Beta Kappa standards in all the areas identified in the past as weaknesses."[66] Congratulations from the higher education community and the press abounded.[67] On the day of the

---

[63] Chris Thompson, *Ole Miss lands Phi Beta Kappa chapter*, CLARION-LEDGER, Oct. 22, 2000, at 1A.

[64] *Id.*

[65] Debbie Rossell, *Phi Beta Kappa says yes to Ole Miss*, OXFORD EAGLE, Oct. 23, 2000, at 1A.

[66] Thompson, *supra* note 22.

[67] *See, e.g., Aiming high: Ole Miss getting Phi Beta Kappa reflects state's greater aspirations*, NE. MISS. DAILY J., Oct. 24, 2000 ("It marks an important step in reaching Khayat's often stated goal for Ole Miss to become recognized as one of the nation's top public universities."); *Education: Phi Beta Kappa award benefits state*, CLARION-

next Ole Miss home football game, a plane flew over Vaught-Hemingway Stadium with a banner floating behind, "Phi Beta Kappa Comes to Ole Miss." Joy, pride, and celebration over this remarkable achievement permeated the air on that homecoming day.[68]

On April 6, 2001, the university held a formal ceremony in the Circle in front of the Lyceum to celebrate the University of Mississippi becoming the first chapter of Phi Beta Kappa at a public university in the State of Mississippi. Designated Beta of Mississippi, the chapter inducted fifty-six students from the top ten percent of those in the College of Liberal Arts as Ole Miss's first class to be given the Golden Key of Phi Beta Kappa.[69] Since that time, Beta of Mississippi has inducted 692 students into its chapter at the University of Mississippi.[70]

Chancellor Khayat made stellar contributions to the University of Mississippi during his fourteen-year tenure as leader of this institution, but none has been larger than his support of the Phi Beta Kappa faculty in their quest to shelter a chapter of the nation's most prestigious academic honor society.[71]

---

LEDGER, Oct. 24, 2000, at 8A ("[T]he PBK decision shows the world that higher education in Mississippi is not only a priority, but an ongoing achievement.").

[68] Warner Alford, former athletic director, described the occasion: "It was like winning the national championship." Lago, *supra* note 5, at 28. Jesse Phillips, publisher of *The Oxford Eagle*, described the occasion as "Ole Miss scores academic 'touchdown.'" Mr. Phillips went on to say: "None of The University's great moments, i.e., a national championship in football, going to the College World Series in baseball or competing in post season play of basketball, tennis or golf, equal The University of Mississippi being tapped by Phi Beta Kappa." Jesse P. Phillips, *Ole Miss scores academic 'touchdown,'* OXFORD EAGLE, Oct. 24, 2000, at 4. Vice Chancellor Gloria Kellum, who had earlier thought Chancellor Khayat was asking for too much too fast with his quest for Phi Beta Kappa, apologized to the chancellor, saying, "When the chapter was approved in Philadelphia, I congratulated him and told him he was courageous. He looked at me and said, 'What about crazy?'" Lago, *supra* note 5, at 24.

[69] Alpha of Mississippi of Phi Beta Kappa was chartered at Millsaps College in 1988 and was the first chapter of the Society in Mississippi. Beta of Mississippi remains the only chapter of Phi Beta Kappa at a public university in this state.

[70] Information on Beta of Mississippi inductees provided by Dr. Luanne Buchanan, Secretary-Treasurer of Beta of Mississippi, May 2-4, 2011.

[71] "Coming just five years after Khayat was named chancellor, the vote is viewed by many across campus, state and nation as the pinnacle of his administration." Lago, *supra* note 5, at 28.

## Dr. Carolyn Ellis Staton*

Having spent the better part of four decades on the Ole Miss campus, Robert Khayat, upon becoming chancellor, already knew all of the university's positives and negatives, nooks and crannies, and successes and failures. His belief in the potential of the university was unparalleled, and he had a keen sense that Ole Miss could be more than a solid state flagship. He knew that with some changes, it could evolve into one of America's great public universities.

Ole Miss had always been a home for Mississippi's gifted students, but Chancellor Khayat set out to make it more attractive to the state's best and brightest students. At the time he became chancellor, Ole Miss's existing honors program was small and had limited resources. He dreamed early that we could offer more to students, and before his investiture, he had already proposed creation of a full-scale honors college to alumni Jim and Sally Barksdale. At his inauguration, he announced the Barksdale gift, then the largest in the history of Ole Miss. There was overwhelming enthusiasm in the Ole Miss community for this endeavor.

And so, with his energy and vision, he created the Sally McDonnell Barksdale Honors College.[72] He put great effort into recruiting the best students, and those efforts were so fruitful that the new Honors College quickly became a dominant part of the

---

* Carolyn Ellis Staton: B.A., Tulane University; M.A., Teacher's College of Columbia University; J.D., Yale Law School. A native of Vicksburg, Mississippi, Dr. Staton served as an assistant U.S. attorney in New Jersey and practiced in a private firm in New York before joining the faculty of the University of Mississippi School of Law in 1977. During the 1993-94 academic year, Dr. Staton served as the acting dean of the law school. In 1994, she was appointed interim associate vice chancellor for academic affairs, and in 1995, associate vice chancellor for academic affairs. In 1999, Dr. Staton became the first female to hold the position of provost and vice chancellor for academic affairs at the University of Mississippi. After Dr. Staton's service at the law school, former students honored her with the creation of an endowed scholarship in her name at the University of Mississippi School of Law. Dr. Staton was the first recipient of the Mississippi Bar Outstanding Woman Lawyer of the Year Award. She has also been the recipient of the Mississippi Bar Susie Blue Buchanan Award.

[72] In 1997, the McDonnell-Barksdale Honors College was created through an endowment made by Jim and Sally Barksdale. After the death of Sally Barksdale in 2003, the honors college was renamed in her honor as the Sally McDonnell Barksdale Honors College. HISTORY OF THE SALLY MCDONNELL BARKSDALE HONORS COLLEGE, http://www.honors.olemiss.edu/about/history/ (last visited Aug. 1, 2011).

culture at Ole Miss. Within short order, students flocked to what he had created, a place that provided education that rivaled the Ivies and other elite private schools, but provided that education in an affordable manner. Today, the Honors College stands as a major achievement, drawing the best students into its community. Students proudly proclaim their identification with the Honors College, and they thrive in the unique opportunities it presents to them.

Chancellor Khayat did not stop with that academic achievement. Through the generosity of the Bancroft Foundation, he created the Croft Institute for International Studies.[73] Aware that universities in Mississippi had little or no courses in international studies, he saw the need to bring students to what has become a global table. Numerous faculty positions were added in new fields, and Asian studies, Latin American studies and Western European studies became established fields of learning. During Khayat's administration, the university went from having no courses relating to Asia to becoming the national flagship program for the study of Chinese.

It has long been known that Ole Miss produced a majority of state and federal political leaders. Building on this history, Chancellor Khayat built the Lott Leadership Institute, which would provide more opportunities for students to learn skills necessary to take on leadership roles, whether in government or the private sector.[74] Along with the Lott Institute, a new major, Public Policy, was created to provide a formal education for future leaders.

While concentrating on the academic community, increasing the size of the library, and bolstering faculty salaries, Chancellor Khayat knew that the road to greatness would take more. With

---

[73] The Croft Institute for International Studies hosts approximately 175 students from twenty-two states and twelve countries. Once in the program, students select a region and global theme on which to concentrate and are required to become proficient in a foreign language. CROFT INSTITUTE FOR INTERNATIONAL STUDIES AT THE UNIVERSITY OF MISSISSIPPI, http://www.croft.olemiss.edu/Pages/?section=5&page=45 (last visited Aug. 1, 2011).

[74] The Lott Leadership Institute has a three-fold mission. First, prepare students to assume positions of leadership. Second, support policy research through the Public Policy Research Center. Third, create and support outreach programs. LOTT LEADERSHIP INSTITUTE, http://www.lottinst.olemiss.edu/About/ (last visited Aug. 1, 2011).

fortitude and vision he led Ole Miss into confronting its past, embracing it, and moving beyond it to become a national leader in racial reconciliation. Thus, the Winter Institute for Racial Reconciliation was created,[75] and the forty-fifth commemoration of James Meredith's admission culminated in the dedication of a statue of Meredith and a reunion of the U.S. Marshals on campus during those turbulent days.

Chancellor Khayat clearly ranks as the most transformative of all Ole Miss chancellors. We often speak of his administration as a renaissance. That is not an understatement. Under his leadership, the University of Mississippi was reborn and became a model for the 21st century American university. His deep love for Ole Miss was the undercurrent for all his achievements, achievements that would dramatically enhance the university while ensuring that it is, indeed, one of America's great public universities.

---

[75] The William Winter Institute for Racial Reconciliation was founded in 1999 to "build more inclusive communities by promoting diversity and citizenship, and by supporting projects that help communities solve local challenges." THE WILLIAM WINTER INSTITUTE FOR RACIAL RECONCILIATION, http://www.winterinstitute.org/pages/aboutus.htm (last visited Aug. 1, 2011).

### Dr. Andrew P. Mullins Jr.*

Nobody loves the University of Mississippi more than Robert Khayat. During his fourteen-year tenure as chancellor, he demonstrated that love every day, and I truly believe that everything he did and each decision he made had the advancement of Ole Miss as the ultimate goal. His love was Ole Miss and his overriding passion was the way it looked—the beauty of the grounds and buildings; the types of flowers in the beds; the lighting of the campus; where the gutters emptied; the lack of paint on the doors and windows; where the air conditioners were located; the design of garbage cans; the height and color of the curbs; the content and color of every campus sign; where grass grew and where it did not and why it did not; the position of the pine straw; the canopy of the trees; the conditions of streets— including the color of pedestrian crossing stripes; and *trash*. To this day if I pass a small piece of litter without picking it up, I feel guilty and have this feeling like God is watching. I appreciate seeing students and faculty members continuing to take pride in the Ole Miss campus just as Robert Khayat instilled in all of us.

Like the rest of campus, his concern for the Grove was always high. On early season football game days, if the weather forecast was for rain, I knew that a call from the chancellor was imminent.[76] It always followed the same pattern—a concern for the soaked grass being trampled beyond repair by the crowds of fans followed by the question of why we don't close the Grove so it will remain in the beautiful condition it was before the season began. My reply was always the same, but painful nevertheless because I could sense the disappointment from one who loved the beauty of the Grove beyond any football fans. My consistent

---

* Dr. Andrew P. Mullins Jr. currently serves as chief of staff to the chancellor and as an associate professor of education. Mullins has served as the special assistant/chief of staff for three chancellors over a seventeen-year span. A native Mississippian, Mullins grew up in Macon, Mississippi before earning a B.A. in history from Millsaps College. Mullins would then earn his M.A. in history from Mississippi College and later attended the University of Mississippi to earn a Ph.D in higher education administration. As a co-founder of the Mississippi Teacher Corps Program, Mullins continues to serve as a co-director for that organization.

[76] Mullins also serves as the chair of the University of Mississippi Game Day Committee, a group responsible for the planning and oversight of activities during game days on the Ole Miss campus.

response was that the grass would be trampled regardless, it would of course be replaced after the season, and we had to serve our fans despite the inclement weather. He would always respond that he knew I would say that, but it was worth a try nevertheless.

All of us who worked with Chancellor Khayat began to see things in a different perspective because of his attention to detail. Now when we visit other campuses, we notice various aspects of appearances that previously would have been overlooked. We all have a deeper appreciation of the small things that make such a difference in a campus—things that collectively contribute to the overall quality of the educational experience. As the appearance of the campus improved, the pride in the university grew. The feelings of those who worked and learned here were that this was indeed a special place. We relished the compliments of visitors and the favorable comparisons with other institutions of higher learning.

It was Chancellor Khayat's love for Ole Miss that prompted his interest in the possibility of a presidential debate being hosted at the university. In 2003, he walked into my office and asked if I knew anything about the presidential debates that had been hosted on university campuses. My reply was that I knew only of a university or two that had hosted in the past. He instructed me to get as much information as possible because he felt that hosting one in the 2004 campaign would be a good way to get our story told to the world. That goal of telling our story, of showing the world that the University of Mississippi had overcome many obstacles and was now a player on the international stage of research universities, would be our focus for the next four years as we learned that the best course of action was to concentrate on the election year of 2008 rather than 2004. The chancellor asked me to begin working on this possibility and promised his full support. The more we discussed the opportunity of telling our story—rising from a small, regional, provincial university with much historical baggage, to a diverse, comprehensive, world class research university—the more excited he became.

When the Commission on Presidential Debates first sent a team of inspectors to Ole Miss, the team members were impressed with the chancellor's commitment. He immediately assured them that we would make every effort necessary. The Commission will not discuss why a site is chosen, and it is all speculation why we were selected in the late fall of 2007 as one of the four sites, but it was obvious the commitment shown by Robert Khayat from that first official visit was a major factor. The amount of money required, the massive physical changes in the campus, and the demands on the staff were daunting at times, but the chancellor's commitment to making it a positive experience for the Ole Miss-Oxford communities never wavered.

There were times when the changes to the campus and to the Ford Center were painful for him to watch—especially when the ugly chain link fence was erected.[77] There were occasions when he would storm into my office and ask why particular changes had to be made. He would offer suggestions for me to give the Secret Service or the Commission staff, but he knew like the suggestion on shutting the Grove for rain on game day, the answer would be the same. However, as the changes fell into place, the chancellor's worries were eased and he increasingly left the details to the Steering Committee while he concentrated on the big picture. He also had the foresight to realize that changes we were required to make for debate day should be made with the future in mind and have positive permanent effects as much as possible.

As the debate day approached he became more at peace and less concerned with the details. He was increasingly pleased with the student and faculty participation and encouraged everyone's involvement. He was confident, calm, and certain the debate would occur even in the midst of the crisis presented by Senator McCain's threat to not show.[78]

Friday, September 26, 2008, went perfectly in every way. One of our most prominent alumni said to me immediately after the

---

[77] In preparation for the debate, the Commission on Presidential Debates required the university to erect fencing around the Ford Center and block nearby roads to protect the safety of presidential candidates John McCain and Barack Obama. Jason Linkins, *Ole Miss Officials: Debate Cancellation Would be $5.5 Million Loss*, HUFFPOST POLITICS (Sept. 24, 2008 5:49 PM), http://www.huffingtonpost.com/2008/09/24/ole-miss-officials-debate_n_129057.html.

[78] Senator John McCain temporarily suspended his campaign in order to focus on congressional negotiations concerning the downturn in the U.S. economy and the proposed Paulson Bailout Package. As a result, McCain requested the debates at Ole Miss be postponed, which worried university officials that he may not attend the scheduled debate. *Id.*

debate, "I have never been prouder of my alma mater as I am tonight." Chancellor Robert Khayat was also filled with pride. The debate was the perfect capstone to the renaissance he had inspired. Due to his leadership, Ole Miss had shown the world the new University of Mississippi.

## J. WARNER ALFORD JR.*

With the help of a young lady named Barbara Jean Hill—a classmate of mine at McComb High—I first met Robert Khayat in 1955 during my senior year of high school. Barbara Jean had an aunt and uncle in Moss Point, whom she would often visit. When Barbara Jean would visit Moss Point, Robert—then the big man on campus at Moss Point High—would show her around town, and they became friends.

Our senior year, Robert and I both signed with Ole Miss to play football. That fall, McComb hosted the South Big-Eight basketball tournament, and Barbara Jean told me Robert was coming to play. She also suggested I talk to him about rooming together at Ole Miss. When I found Robert during a break in play, I said, "Look, Barbara Jean says we ought to room together at Ole Miss," to which he replied 'Yeah, I guess she's right." That's how Robert and I met and started a friendship that flourished during our college years and remains today. That friendship has allowed me to view Robert's greatest triumphs, but has also provided me with a glimpse of his resiliency and his ability to overcome all obstacles and setbacks that he encounters.

Most people do not know that Robert planned to become a doctor when he enrolled at Ole Miss. In fact, he came to Oxford the summer before his freshman year to take a Chemistry class, so he wouldn't have to take it while playing football in the fall. His teacher was C.M. Jones, better known to his students as "Cyanide Jones." Robert told me that Jones covered everything he had learned in Chemistry at Moss Point High in the first ten minutes of his college class. When "Cyanide" handed grades out at the end of the term, Robert got a D.

---

* J. Warner Alford Jr.: B.B.A., University of Mississippi; M.A., University of Mississippi. Alford, a native of McComb, Mississippi, served as a captain of the Rebels' 1960 SEC and National Championship football team. A guard on the Rebels' offensive line, Alford was inducted into the Ole Miss Sports and the Mississippi Sports Halls of Fame. Following his playing career, Alford returned to Ole Miss to serve as defensive line coach under Head Coach Billy Kinard. In 1978, Alford was hired as the University of Mississippi athletic director and held that position until 1994. From 1994 to 2004 Alford served as an executive in the insurance industry, before returning to Ole Miss in 2004 to lead the Ole Miss Alumni Association as its executive director. Alford is married to the former Kay Swayze, and the couple has three children and six grandchildren.

He was determined to do better the next semester, but after the first, he knew he needed help. So Robert went to talk to Cyanide Jones and said, "Dr. Jones, I really need some help in this class." Jones agreed, saying, "I think we can get you through this class, but if you pass, I want you to promise me you will never step foot in the Chemistry building again." Robert agreed and eventually did pass, but I always liked to say that Jones' Chemistry class ended Robert's hope of becoming a doctor, at least of medicine.

While at Ole Miss, Robert was a star athlete in two sports. He played baseball for Coach Tom Swayze and football for Coach John Vaught. As the Rebels' catcher, he helped lead Ole Miss to back-to-back SEC Championships in 1959 and 1960. As the Rebels' kicker, he led the nation in scoring by a kicker in 1958 and 1959. He also earned Academic All-American and All-SEC honors in 1959. All of those accolades, however, would not have been possible had Robert not had the resiliency he possessed.

Early in his college career, in 1958, we played the University of Tennessee in Knoxville. We had never beaten Tennessee in Knoxville, ever, but we were playing pretty good that game. We were up 16-12 after the half, but the lead didn't last long. Tennessee had a little back named Gene Etter, who broke a long run, and they went up 18-16. Then we got the ball and started driving down field. We moved the ball all the way to the 19-yard line, and all Robert had to do was kick a field goal to win the game—but Robert missed. A kick he had probably made a million times, but this time he was off the mark.

That miss tore him up. When we got back to campus, Robert told me he was going to the stadium. I asked if he wanted me to go with him, but he said, "No, I'll take Bill Keys." Bill, who was manager of our team, tells the story of how they went to the stadium, and he held the ball on the 19-yard line, while Robert kicked and kicked and kicked. Robert tells me he sometimes wakes up in the middle of the night and still thinks about missing that kick.

Robert's determination paid off, and after graduation the Washington Redskins drafted him in the NFL draft. He kicked for them, and even went to the Pro Bowl his rookie year. It was a golden year for Robert, and it appeared that everything was going great. During the offseason, however, he went to Vicksburg to do his practice teaching, as he was planning on teaching high school after his football career. It was during that time, in the summer of 1961, that he developed pancreatitis. It was terrible. Robert's family was called to the hospital several times and told he wasn't going to make it, but like every other tough situation he has faced, he overcame it. He eventually went back home to Moss Point to recover, but he often says that he left Mercy Hospital in an ambulance, "but it could have been a hearse." Not only did Robert overcome his life-threatening illness, but he returned to the NFL and continued his pro career.

Robert's perseverance would earn him induction into the Ole Miss Athletics Hall of Fame and the Mississippi Sports Hall of Fame. During the Ole Miss Football Centennial in 1993, fans chose him as the kicker on the "Team of the Century." He also received the NFL Lifetime Achievement Award in 1998 and the National Football Foundation and College Hall of Fame's Distinguished American Award in 2003.

Following his pro career, Robert returned to our beloved Ole Miss to attend law school, where he graduated third in his class in 1966. Robert loved it so much that three years later he joined the law school's faculty. He took a short leave of absence during the 1980-1981 academic year to earn a master of laws at Yale University before returning home to Ole Miss to teach once again. Robert then ascended to the position of associate dean of the law school before moving to the lyceum to serve as vice chancellor in 1984. In 1989, Robert became the first president of the NCAA Foundation, a position he held for three years, but was once again called back to his post as a law professor at Ole Miss.

In 1993, the Ole Miss Law School was looking for a dean. Robert absolutely loves Ole Miss and the school of law, and he wanted nothing more than to be dean, but the faculty voted him unacceptable. Robert was incredibly hurt. I remember telling him, "Look, I think God has something better for you. Your time will come." I had no idea how prophetic those words would be. Two years later, the Board of Trustees of Institutions of Higher Learning selected Robert to be the university's chancellor. The rest, as they say, is history. His legendary accomplishments as chancellor are well-documented and would not have been possible had it not been for Robert's unwillingness to give up.

When Robert and I were playing football for Ole Miss, there was a 25-second play clock, meaning that if somebody knocked you on your keister or rang your bells so to speak, you had 25 seconds to shake it off, get back up, and get yourself back into the game. We called that the 25-second rule and Robert applied it to every aspect of his life both on and off the field. He refused to let difficulties or disappointments keep him down for long. It is why he has always bounced back, whether from missing a kick, illness, getting passed over as dean, or receiving letters and calls from people who wanted the university to halt its progress. Robert Khayat refuses to give up or be deterred by setbacks.

While he was chancellor, there were many challenges and obstacles that could have hindered his progress. But, just as he did in his personal life, Robert applied the 25-second rule and overcame them. As a result, Ole Miss improved academically and athletically, and it truly became the great public university that he envisioned.

Everyone knows of Robert's love for people and his affection for Ole Miss. As chancellor, he called members of the Ole Miss community his "family." Those of us who know him well know how much he meant those words. He believed in Ole Miss, and he wouldn't accept the thought that we, as a family, couldn't achieve our goal of becoming a great public university.

That resiliency is embedded in his character. Robert is able to make people believe in themselves and he inspires people to be better than they thought they could be. Others didn't start believing this really was a great university until they witnessed how much Robert Khayat believed in the university and how much he was willing to overcome to move the university forward. One of Robert's greatest goals was securing a Phi Beta Kappa chapter for Ole Miss. Achieving that goal was like winning the national championship and making the game-winning kick. No one believed we could win, but Robert went after it, and he achieved it. As long as I've known him, when he sets his mind to achieving something, he does whatever it takes to achieve that goal.

The University of Mississippi is better because of Robert's love, service, and vision for making it a great university. He lived and fulfilled his dream for Ole Miss through his dynamic leadership, which he learned on the playing field. That's where he learned the benefits of teamwork and developed his never-quit attitude. As chancellor, he built a leadership team that loved him and Ole Miss, and then he gave us the ball and let us run with it. Because we believed in him and believed in what he wanted to accomplish, there wasn't anything we couldn't do. When the game-ending buzzer sounded, Robert and his team had transformed the entire university.

It is a fitting symbol of his love and his resolve that the school that once voted him unacceptable as its dean now finds itself housed in a building bearing his name.

## Chancellor Daniel W. Jones*

When Robert C. Khayat announced his retirement as chancellor two years ago, many of us were deeply shaken. We simply could not imagine Ole Miss without him at its helm, because it was he who inspired us to accomplish more than we ever dreamed we could, and we treasured the years we were privileged to work with him. Few loved the university and its people more, or better, than he did, and it was that love that inspired him, and us, to work to build Ole Miss into a great university worthy of admiration and respect.

Chancellor Khayat's deep affection for Ole Miss began as a student, when he was a catcher for baseball coach Tom Swayze and a kicker and lineman for legendary football coach John Vaught. Since then, that affection, coupled with his ability to enable people to believe in themselves and what they are doing, has sparked a multitude of achievements that faculty, staff, students, and alumni believed impossible.

Those of us in the Ole Miss community caught our first glimpse of that love when he was invested as chancellor. He began his tenure by shoring up academic programs. He did so by sharing his vision for academic excellence with others and enlisting their help to significantly increase endowments, library holdings, technological resources, liberal arts programs, and student scholarships. Shortly afterward, university faculty secured a Phi Beta Kappa chapter, the first awarded to a public university in Mississippi.

Chancellor Khayat demonstrated this love and commitment many times during his fourteen years as our CEO. On his watch,

---

* Daniel W. Jones, M.D., is the 16th chancellor of the University of Mississippi. Prior to his appointment on July 1, 2009, Dr. Jones was vice chancellor for health affairs, dean of the school of medicine, and Herbert G. Langford professor of medicine at the University of Mississippi Medical Center (UMMC) in Jackson. Active in the American Heart Association (AHA), Dr. Jones served as national president of the organization from 2007 to 2008. A native Mississippian, he graduated from Mississippi College in 1971 and earned his M.D. in 1975 at the University of Mississippi Medical Center. Upon completion of his residency, he maintained a private practice in Laurel, Mississippi. A fellow of the American College of Physicians, Dr. Jones is certified by the American Board of Internal Medicine and is designated as a specialist in clinical hypertension by the American Society of Hypertension Specialists. He has been named one of the "Best Doctors in America" from 1996 to 2008 and is a member of Alpha Omega Alpha national honor medical society.

Ole Miss conducted two capital campaigns that raised nearly $775 million. With the help of thousands of donors, the university created its top-notch Sally McDonnell Barksdale Honors College, Lott Leadership Institute, Croft Institute for International Studies, and Galtney Center for Academic Computing. The university also produced two Rhodes Scholars, rose in the national rankings, and hosted a presidential debate. All of these accomplishments, and others, reflect Chancellor Khayat's ability to share his affection and vision for the university with all of those around him.

Chancellor Khayat has been a dedicated caretaker. He left the university a foundation that includes one of the country's most beautiful and well-maintained campuses, an annual operating budget of nearly $1.5 billion, and a legacy of securing more than $170 million worth of research each year, and providing some $138 million annually in financial aid to deserving students. Under his transformational leadership, Ole Miss invested more than $535 million in physical facilities on the Oxford and Jackson campuses. On the Oxford campus, these facilities include a new performing arts center, chapel, business and accountancy complex, eight-story Inn at Ole Miss, indoor practice facility, academic support center, residential college, and office buildings for the athletics and physical plant departments. At the University of Mississippi Medical Center in Jackson, new facilities include a new university hospital, student union, research center, health-related professions building, and new critical care, children's, and women and infants hospitals.

Few people have done more to enhance the university, and certainly no one could have asked for more effort, diligence, love, and ability than we received from Robert Khayat. Chancellor Khayat was never shy about telling members of the university family that they have a responsibility to move our university and state forward. His increased expectations lifted every part of the university, and that has led to greater expectations throughout our state. During my time at the Medical Center, he encouraged us to expand our vision and role in addressing health disparities in our state and nation. Like many others, I simply couldn't say, "No" whenever he asked for my help, and working with him is a rare privilege.

We believed in him and believed in what he wanted to accomplish for our university, so we gave to Ole Miss, or we gave our best for her. It could be said that Chancellor Khayat created and coached his own legendary team of Ole Miss faculty, staff, students, alumni, and friends. We are privileged to have been a part of that team.

Our former provost once said that Ole Miss was relatively unknown before Robert Khayat became its chancellor, but was much more nationally prominent when he retired in 2009.[79] Chancellor Khayat did, indeed, change the university's direction, and I, too, think history will treat him as one of the heroes of Ole Miss. I say that because I watched his efforts to make his alma mater blind to color and warm and welcoming to all. Under his leadership, the university commemorated the fortieth anniversary of its integration, erected a civil rights monument, and established the William Winter Institute for Racial Reconciliation. By the time he retired, Chancellor Khayat had helped create a model of reconciliation and a university culture that values and respects the dignity of everyone.

When Chancellor Khayat retired nearly two years ago, he said he was doing so "with a heart filled with gratitude to the thousands of people who support our university" and "with an abiding affection for the people and the school."[80] We, on the other hand, will always be thankful for his many years of leadership and service. Many of us have tried over the years to express our gratitude and our affection for him. But those efforts fell short of the appreciation Robert Khayat is owed. We have inducted him into our Athletics Hall of Fame, chosen him as the kicker for our "Team of the Century" and our Outstanding Law Professor of the Year, and established scholarships in his name. Now we are immensely proud to place the name Robert C. Khayat upon this school's magnificent new law center not only to ensure that his contributions to Ole Miss are remembered by future generations,

---

[79] *Chancellor Announces Retirement Plans: Robert Khayat to Retire June 30, After 14 years Shepherding Ole Miss*, (Jan. 6, 2009), http://news.olemiss.edu/index.php?option=com_content&view=article&id=4287%3Akhayatretirement&catid=124%3Anewsdesk1arc&Itemid=10.

[80] *Id.*

but also to inspire them to accomplish more than they ever dreamed they could.

*Robert Khayat played catcher for the Ole Miss Rebels baseball team

*As a result of his success on the football field, Robert Khayat was selected as the placekicker on the Ole Miss "Team of the Century"

*The Washington Redskins drafted Robert Khayat in the 1960 National Football League draft

*Robert Khayat served as the Redskins' starting kicker for three years

*Professor Khayat lecturing first-year law students in what is now Farley Hall

*Associate Dean Khayat at work in his office at the Lamar Law Center

*Chancellor Khayat leads students on a walk through campus

*Chancellor Khayat at work in his office in the Lyceum

*Chancellor Emeritus Khayat in the new Robert C. Khayat Law Center

*Chancellor Emeritus Khayat with wife Margaret, daughter Margaret Khayat Bratt and her husband David, son Robert C. Khayat, Jr., and his wife Susannah Baker Khayat, and the Khayat's grandchildren Molly, Ben, and Betsey